Lighted
Scroll Saw Projects

Sue Mey

Schiffer Publishing Ltd

4880 Lower Valley Road · Atglen, PA · 19310

Other Schiffer Books on Related Subjects
The Scroll Saw Book, 0-88740-774-9, $12.95
Scroll Sawing in Metal: Patterns and Techniques, 0-7643-1564-1, $14.95
Incredible Stackables: Ornamental Scroll Saw Projects, 0-7643-1304-5, $14.95

Schiffer Books are available at special discounts for bulk purchases for sales promotions or premiums. Special editions, including personalized covers, corporate imprints, and excerpts can be created in large quantities for special needs. For more information contact the publisher:

Published by Schiffer Publishing Ltd.
4880 Lower Valley Road
Atglen, PA 19310
Phone: (610) 593-1777; Fax: (610) 593-2002
E-mail: Info@schifferbooks.com

For the largest selection of fine reference books on this and related subjects, please visit our web site at:
www.schifferbooks.com
We are always looking for people to write books on new and related subjects. If you have an idea for a book please contact us at the above address.

This book may be purchased from the publisher.
Include $5.00 for shipping.
Please try your bookstore first.
You may write for a free catalog.

In Europe, Schiffer books are distributed by
Bushwood Books
6 Marksbury Ave.
Kew Gardens
Surrey TW9 4JF England
Phone: 44 (0) 20 8392 8585; Fax: 44 (0) 20 8392 9876
E-mail: info@bushwoodbooks.co.uk
Website: www.bushwoodbooks.co.uk

Disclaimer and acknowledgment of trademarks
Most of the items and products in this book may be covered by various copyrights, trademarks, and logotypes. Their use herein is for identification purposes only. All rights are reserved by their respective owners. The text and products pictured in this book are from the collection of the author, its publisher, or various private collectors. This book is not sponsored, endorsed, or otherwise affiliated with any of the companies whose products are represented herein. They include Rustins, Ltd., Barloworld Plascon, Den Braven Sealants, Rekara Mills Pty Ltd., and Henkel SA Pty Ltd. This book is derived from the author's independent research.

Copyright © 2010 by Sue Mey
*Unless otherwise noted, all photos are the property of the author.
Library of Congress Control Number: 2009936375

All rights reserved. No part of this work may be reproduced or used in any form or by any means—graphic, electronic, or mechanical, including photocopying or information storage and retrieval systems—without written permission from the publisher.
The scanning, uploading and distribution of this book or any part thereof via the Internet or via any other means without the permission of the publisher is illegal and punishable by law. Please purchase only authorized editions and do not participate in or encourage the electronic piracy of copyrighted materials.
"Schiffer," "Schiffer Publishing Ltd. & Design," and the "Design of pen and ink well" are registered trademarks of Schiffer Publishing Ltd.

Designed by RoS
Type set in Humanst521 BT

ISBN: 978-0-7643-3386-6
Printed in China

Dedication

For Natalie, the light of my life,
and Donnie, my soul mate.

Thank you both for your unwavering patience and support while I single-mindedly pursued the realization of my dream.

Acknowledgments

There are several people I would like to thank. Paps, for allowing me to get in the way in his workshop from an early age and planting the seed of my enthusiasm for woodworking, and Mams, for her interest and constant encouragement in everything that I do. Also Dee and Peet, for their interest and support.

The late Judith Mattard, fondly known as The Lumberlady, for her sharp wit, loyal friendship, and introduction to hardwoods I had never heard of before. I also thank Shannon Flowers, editorial manager of *Scroll Saw Woodworking & Crafts®*, for giving me my first break in 2005, and Bob Duncan, technical editor, for his infallible editing skills; Robert Becker, editor of *Creative Woodworks & Crafts®*, for his continued support of my work, and Debbie McGowan, managing editor, for being such a ray of sunshine and always knowing just what it is that I am trying to put across; Vernon and Kari Brown of *The Wooden Teddy Bear®*, for their support by marketing my designs; and Warren Schmidt of *The Home Handyman®* and Marichen van Zyl of *Craftwise®*, for publishing and promoting my work in South Africa.

Fellow scroller and friend, David de May, for taking the time to read the manuscript and giving his input. Scroll sawyers from around the world for their support, messages of appreciation for my magazine articles and website patterns, and constant requests and suggestions for new designs. You keep me on my toes and ensure that I continue to grow and strive to make good quality patterns.

Lastly but by no means the least, I am grateful to Schiffer Publishing and the late Peter B. Schiffer, for choosing to publish my first book, and to my editors, Jeff Snyder and Jennifer Marie Savage, for being so friendly and helpful to me in this endeavor.

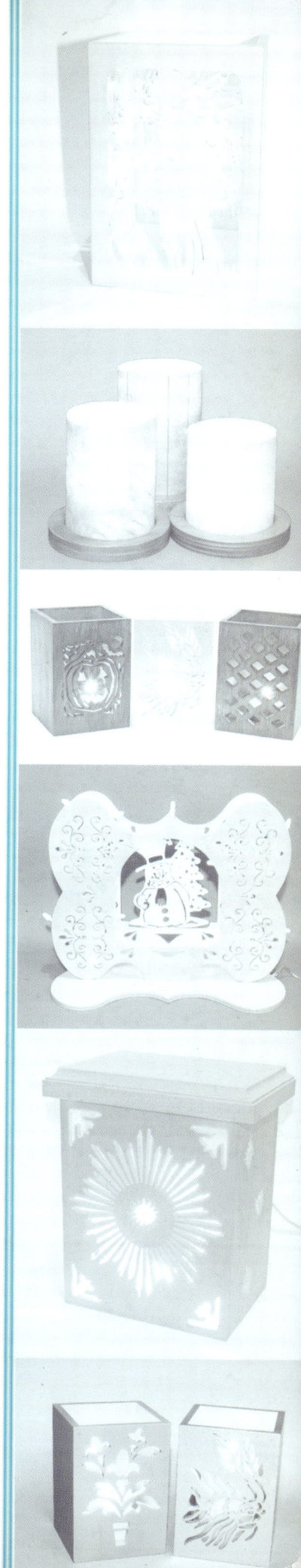

Measurement Conversion Chart

Inches to millimeters (mm) and centimeters (cm)

Inches	mm	cm
1/8	3	0.3
1/4	6	0.6
3/8	10	1.0
1/2	13	1.3
5/8	16	1.6
3/4	19	1.9
7/8	22	2.2
1	25	2.5
1 1/4	32	3.2
1 1/2	38	3.8
1 3/4	44	4.4
2	51	5.1
2 1/2	64	6.4
3	76	7.6

Contents

Introduction 6

Chapter 1: **Basic Procedures, Tips, & Techniques**
- 1.1 Safety Guidelines 7
- 1.2 Material Selection and Preparation 8
- 1.3 Pattern Attachment 10
- 1.4 Saw Preparation 10
- 1.5 Blade Selection 11
- 1.6 Drilling Blade Entry Holes 12
- 1.7 Making Cuts 13
- 1.8 Assembling & Finishing the Project 16
- 1.9 Lighting Options 20

Chapter 2: **Luminaries**
- 2.1 Tall Luminary 22
- 2.2 Fairy Luminary 24
- 2.3 Assorted Luminaries 27
- 2.4 Acrylic Luminary 31
- 2.5 Square Paper Luminary 33
- 2.6 Round Paper Luminaries 35

Chapter 3: **Nightlights**
- 3.1 Cherubs Nightlight 38
- 3.2 Fairy on Moon Nightlight 43
- 3.3 Pine Cones Nightlight 47
- 3.4 Bright Sun Nightlight 50
- 3.5 Decorative Fret Nightlight 53

Chapter 4: **Table Lamps**
- 4.1 Lighthouse Lamp 57
- 4.2 Lamp with Overlays 64

Chapter 5: **Candle Stands and Sconce**
- 5.1 Dolphin Votive Stand 71
- 5.2 Nativity Candle Stand 74
- 5.3 Cross Sconce 77
- 5.4 Compound-Cut Candle Stand 79
- 5.5 Patio Candle Lamp 83

Chapter 6: **Layered Projects**
- 6.1 Layered Arch 90
- 6.2 Layered Pyramid 94
- 6.3 Layered Christmas Tree 96
- 6.4 Layered Snowman 98

Chapter 7: **Decorative Touches**
- 7.1 Lighted Mantle Clock 103
- 7.2 Lighted Christmas Presents 112

Gallery 117

Introduction

Scroll sawing is a wonderful, rewarding, and easy woodworking hobby with which to get started. It brings you a true and immediate sense of accomplishment. When compared to all other power-driven devices that cut wood, the scroll saw is unquestionably the safest, most user-friendly, and easiest to master. It requires no mechanical skills and it allows for safely cutting small pieces of wood to quickly make a variety of projects. The intricate pieces you can create with a scroll saw range from inlay work to marquetry to fine fretwork. Jewelry, ornaments, toys, and artistic woodworking pieces can be made, and, once you start scroll sawing, you will quickly gain experience and want to try all the various aspects like Intarsia, segmentation, relief-cutting, and 3-D scrolling.

Over the years, I have practiced various arts and crafts and have always been a hands-on person. When I glimpsed a scroll saw for the first time at a woodworking show about fifteen years ago, my interest was piqued. I stood watching people intently bent over their saws, turning out amazing pieces of art in wood, and knew it was something I wanted to try. I acquired my first scroll saw soon afterwards. As I did not have a workshop, it was promptly set up on one of my kitchen counters. In preparation, I had bought some 1" pine and Patrick Spielman's book *Scroll Saw Basics*. Ten minutes later I had completed my first stand-up animal puzzle. I had failed to keep to the pattern lines I had drawn, and the puzzle pieces would only push out towards the back, but I was thoroughly hooked on a hobby that was to become my passion and finally, my occupation. A spare room was swiftly converted to a workshop, and easels, palettes, and other craft supplies were put away in favor of power tools.

Since then I have come to learn that it is not always as simple as it appears in handbooks. The true nature of scroll sawing is an arduous process of constant learning, with the infinite highs of new discoveries and the despondency when projects do not quite work out as proposed in the teachings. It was a combination of the former and the latter that ignited my eagerness to learn all there was to know and which eventually led to designing my own patterns for projects. I also discovered that by studying different disciplines of working with wood and borrowing from these, I could combine the knowledge attained to make scroll sawing not only interesting, but diverse and colorful as well. In doing so, I broke away from mere pattern cutting to take my craft to new heights.

Some time ago a fellow scroller suggested that I make some designs for Schwibbogen, the traditional German lighted arches. This led to other layered projects in the form of pyramids and trees. I subsequently warmed up to the theme of lighted scroll saw projects and added nightlights, luminaries, and candle stands to the collection and the result is the project variety combined in this book.

Basic Procedures, Tips, and Techniques

There are several processes associated with scroll sawing. This chapter will take you through these procedures, from working safely, to choosing the material for your project, to assembling the work pieces and finishing the item.

1.1 Safety Guidelines

Using Scroll Saws & Other Power Tools

- Wear a dust mask while working with the scroll saw, especially if a dust blower is used instead of a vacuum.
- Wear a face mask when cutting glass or metal.
- Wear eye and ear protection when working with power tools. It is tempting not to use eye gear when you are working with a scroll saw. Be safe and err on the side of caution.
- Protective goggles are essential when cutting acrylics, glass, or metal.
- Never allow fingers to come near any moving blades or cutters.
- When cutting very small pieces of wood, attach them to a larger backing of cardboard or scrap plywood to help control the wood and ensure that your fingers are away from the blade.
- Wear appropriate attire. Loose sleeves, ties, scarves, and loose hair can get in the way and pose a danger when working with power tools. Do not wear jewelry.
- Do not allow yourself to be distracted or your mind to wander when using power tools or sharp objects. Most accidents in the workshop happen when a woodworker is tired or when his or her attention is focused elsewhere. Never work when tired, in a hurry, or not in the mood. Use common sense at all times.
- Never work under the influence of drugs, alcohol, or medicine.
- Children should only be allowed to use a scroll saw under supervision.
- Ensure that the work area is well ventilated. It is preferable to connect a vacuum or dust extractor to the extraction port of your scroll saw.
- Before removing dust and chips from the scroll saw and other power tools, ensure the machine is switched off and unplugged.
- In case of a power failure, return the power switch to the OFF position.

Chapter 1

1.1 Safety Guidelines

1.2 Material Selection and Preparation

1.3 Pattern Attachment

1.4 Saw Preparation

1.5 Blade Selection

1.6 Drilling Entry Holes

1.7 Making Cuts

1.8 Assembling & Finishing the Project

1.9 Lighting Options

1.2 Material Selection and Preparation

Selection of Materials

Wood

Careful selection of the type of material you will use is very important for the final outcome of your project.

Wood products suitable for scroll sawing include various solid woods and wood sheet materials like plywood and MDF (Medium Density Fiberboard). Particle board, also known as chipboard, is *not* suitable for scroll sawing.

Hardwoods come in various species, colors, and grain patterns, and are more attractive than plywood. However, they are more expensive and also time consuming, as they require more sanding. Hardwood finishes beautifully, though they are also more likely to warp.

Plywood, on the other hand, is less expensive, requires less sanding, and has the standard thickness needed. It is also less likely to develop cracks or warp. The commercial grades of plywood often have voids in between the layers, making it less ideal for scrolling. Purchase only the best quality plywood available.

MDF is stable, less expensive, easy to cut, and suitable for painted or stained projects. I like to use partridge wood, maple, African mahogany, and blonde mahogany (also referred to as white lauan). I have been fortunate to work with exotic woods such as Brazilian cherry, snake wood, and zebra wood. Oak, cherry, and rose wood char easily and you need to slow down your saw and change blades more often when cutting these woods.

For the beginner scroller, I would suggest woods like Jacaranda, red cedar, and poplar, which cut easily and finish well. Softwood, like clear pine, is also a good choice if you choose to paint your project. Be sure the wood you choose is free of knots. Try to obtain off cuts of solid wood, plywood, and MDF from a furniture manufacturer or cabinetmaker while you practice your skills on the scroll saw.

Always try to find and use wood with a nice grain pattern and a lot of character. Regardless of how expensive the wood is, your finished project will be seen and felt for years to come, so use the best material you can afford when making a special project.

Acrylic

Acrylic is stable and is available in various colors and thicknesses. Acrylic is generally manufactured in two forms namely cell cast sheet and extruded sheet. Some differences exist between cast and extruded acrylic properties due to their molecular structure and this can be reflected in their fabrication behaviour. It is suitable to replace glass in projects, can be used for two dimensional pieces like plaques and ornaments, as well as three dimensional projects like the luminaries in *Chapter Two* and the Christmas boxes in *Chapter Seven*.

Keep the protective masking film of the acrylic in place when using it for a project and only remove it before assembly, if applicable. This reduces the likelihood of scratching the material and keeps it free of finger marks. Acrylic is cleaned by washing with cold water to which a little detergent has been added. The use of solvents such as turpentine, white spirit, or mentholated spirit is not recommended.

Most power tools can be used on acrylics. For drilling holes in acrylic, high-speed steel or tungsten carbide tipped drill bits are preferable to achieve a good finish.

Acrylic can be bonded using special adhesives made for the type of acrylic used. To assemble three-dimensional projects, strips of masking tape are essential to keep the pieces in place not only while you line them up, but also while the adhesive is drying. The drying time for different acrylic adhesives vary and can be as long as twenty-four to forty-eight hours.

A selection of attractive hardwoods. From the left is partridge wood, rosewood, zebrano, wild olive, black ivory, red ivory, teak, and blonde mahogany.

Various types of plywood with MDF on the right.

Patterns are attached directly onto the protective masking film with spray adhesive or a glue stick.

If the masking film has lifted in places, cover the acrylic with a layer of masking tape.

A lower speed and feed rate are required when cutting the material, as it softens and melts from the heat generated by the saw blade.

If preferred, acrylic can be stacked on top of scrap plywood. It can also be sandwiched between two layers of plywood. This method reduces the problem of the plastic melting and the result is a clean and smooth cut surface.

A disc sander may be used to sand the straight edges of acrylic, and only light pressure should be applied to prevent softening or melting of the material. Acrylic becomes brittle once cooled down, so after cutting or sanding, edges may be carefully wiped to remove stray bits. Use 500-grit sandpaper or a soft cloth for this purpose. Use regular fine-tooth scroll saw blades that are not dull.

Material Preparation

Sanding

Use a palm sander or a random orbital sander to sand the wood. This reduces the amount of hand sanding to be done later as well as the risk of breaking fragile pieces when the sanding is done after cutting. Start with 50 grit, which is the roughest, then 80 grit, followed by 120 grit and 180 grit, and ending with 320 grit sandpaper, which is the finest. If the wood is planed and has no mill marks or blemishes, the sanding stages with very rough sandpaper are not necessary. Remove sanding dust with a clean paintbrush, lint free cloth, or an air compressor.

Stacking and Wood Thickness

Use small pieces of thin double sided tape to secure the layers for stack cutting.

Secure the layers for stack cutting with hot glue on the four sides of the stack.

Stack cutting allows you to make several identical pieces at once. Work pieces can be stacked for disc sanding or cutting. My method of choice is to place small pieces of thin, double-sided tape between the layers, positioning them in waste areas of the design. Other methods for securing the layers are to apply hot glue or painter's tape on the four sides of the stack, or to wrap the stack in layers of clear packing tape, making sure the pattern is still visible. These methods work best if the work pieces are all the same size. Finally, panel pins or thin nails can be inserted through the layers, again making sure that they are placed in waste areas of the design. Be careful that the pins or nails do not protrude all the way to the bottom of the stack because the sharp ends will scratch your saw table and prevent the work piece from moving freely as you cut.

If wood of a required thickness is not available, two pieces of thinner wood can be laminated face-to-face. Ensure the surfaces of the wood pieces are smooth and free of dust. Apply an even, thin coat of wood glue to the meeting surfaces, stack the pieces, and apply clamps to the entire surface. Similarly, a wider work piece is obtained by edge-gluing two pieces of wood. Do not apply the clamps so tightly that most of the glue is squeezed out of the joint. Excess glue is removed using a damp cloth. Once the glue has dried, the wood is sanded using a palm sander or a random orbital sander.

Cut the material to the approximate size required for your pattern.

If the wood is uneven and has visible mill marks, it is sanded before the pattern is applied.

The stack can also be wrapped in layers of clear packing tape, either directly on the wood or on top of the pattern.

Two pieces of 1/8" plywood can be laminated to obtain material where 1/4" wood is required.

Pieces of wood are laminated for a 2.6" thick work piece.

1.3 Pattern Attachment

Photocopy or scan and print the pattern, enlarging or reducing it to the desired size. Cover the surface of the work piece with masking tape. Apply temporary bond spray adhesive to the back of the pattern, working outside or in a well-ventilated area. Place scrap paper or newsprint under the pattern. Spray a generous amount of glue onto the paper; do not spray it on the wood. Wait for approximately thirty seconds, position the pattern on the tape, and press down in a few places. Starting in the center and working your way to the sides, smooth out the pattern by hand to remove any air bubbles. Work gently so as not to tear the pattern. Glue stick does not hold the pattern as well as spray glue, but can be used for more simple patterns without many inside cuts. A method that eliminates the need for glue is to print the pattern on a full sheet label. The backing of the label paper is removed and the pattern is stuck onto the wood. Simple patterns without a lot of detail can be transferred onto the wood using carbon paper and a stylus, or an old ballpoint pen. Attach one end of the pattern to the wood with masking tape to keep it from moving during transfer.

Use scissors to remove the excess paper up to approximately 1/8" beyond the perimeter line of the pattern.

To allow for easy removal of the pattern after cutting, cover the surface of the work piece with masking tape or blue painter's tape. The application of a tape layer keeps the glue off the wood so that you do not have to soak the pattern with mineral spirit afterwards or apply heat to remove it.

To prevent tear-out on the underside when cutting a project, or to reduce the burrs on the bottom of your project, attach some carton paper or scrap wood as a bottom layer. Strips of thin double-sided tape can be used to attach the disposable layer.

> **WHEN** cutting wood that burns easily — like oak, cherry, and rosewood — wrap the whole work piece with clear packing tape so that it is both on top of the pattern and at the bottom of the work piece. The packing tape helps to lubricate the blade and prevents charring in the cuts

1.4 Saw Preparation

Before using your scroll saw for the first time, read and review the owner's manual and observe all of the safety precautions relative to the use of the scroll saw.

The saw is placed on a stand or bench. A heavy welded stand is best as it helps to absorb any vibration. Your saw and stand should be placed on a solid surface. If placed on a wooden floor, the saw may tend to vibrate and be noisy. If you prefer to sit while you cut, choose a comfortable stool at an appropriate height.

To install your blade, make sure the teeth are facing you and pointing downward. A blade installed backwards won't cut wood and an upside down blade will pick the wood up off the table bed and slap it back down again. You will notice sawdust and burrs on the top surface of your work piece instead of the bottom, if the blade is upside down. With very fine teeth, it is hard to see the direction of the teeth. Before installing a fine tooth blade, simply run your index finger lightly up and down along the front of the blade to make sure the teeth are pointing down. For proper blade tension, insert the blade and turn the tension knob three-quarters of a turn past the point of resistance. A blade that is too loose will not cut a straight pattern line, and a blade that is too tight will break.

For most projects, it is necessary to make cuts with the saw table set square to the blade. The factory calibrations of the blade tilt-scales of most scroll saws are difficult to read and the majority of them are not accurate. Use a small square or protractor to make and check this adjustment. Another method to test it would be to make a 1/2" long cut straight into a piece of 3/4" wood. Reverse the blade out of the cut. Turn the wood over and, with the saw turned off, reinsert the blade in the same cut. If it slides in easily, the table is square. Make sure you check this regularly, especially if you occasionally cut on an angle.

Most saws have a dust blower that blows the dust towards the scroller. A fan can be placed on the left side of the saw to blow the dust to the right and away from you. It is preferable to connect a dust extractor or vacuum to the extraction port. Remove the blower tube from the back of the bellows and insert it in the extraction porthole. Although a dust extractor can be noisy, it is an excellent way to minimize dust in your work area.

Use a small square or a protractor to make sure the saw table is set square to the blade.

1.5 Blade Selection

Use a suitable blade as dictated by the wood thickness, amount of cutting detail, and sharp radius turns required. The standard scroll saw blade is five inches long. Less expensive saws often use pin end blades. These blades restrict the intricacy of internal cuts one is able to make, as a fairly large drill hole is required for the pin to fit through. Pin blades are also not available in the narrow, fine tooth options. The ideal blade is pin-less. They are also known as flat end blades or plain end blades and are secured in blade clamps.

Scroll saw blades come in many sizes and styles. Sizes are designated by numbers and range from No. 2/0 and No. 0 in very fine, No. 1, No. 2, No. 3, and No. 4 in fine, No. 5 and No. 7 in medium, and No. 8 to No. 12 in larger sizes. A general rule is to use wider blades with fewer teeth for sawing larger curves and cutting thicker woods and to use narrower blades with more teeth for intricate details in thin woods. Harder substances require larger teeth. A very complex pattern will require a blade with small teeth. Here are some guidelines:

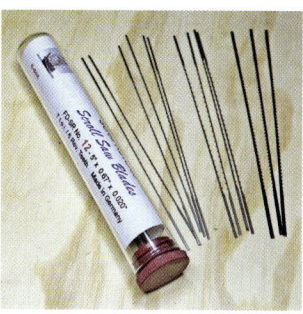

A selection of flat end blades.

- No. 2/0 or No. 1 for 1/8" wood
- No. 2 or No. 3 for 1/4" to 1/2" wood
- No. 5, No. 7, and No. 9 for 3/4" to 1" wood
- No. 12 for wood thicker than 1"

Major Blade Types

Standard tooth blades

The teeth are all the same size and distance apart. The two major kinds are wood blades and metal blades. Hardened steel is used to make metal blades and they have much smaller teeth with less space between them. Wood blades have larger teeth with more space between them, for clearing the sawdust as you cut.

Skip tooth blades

These are similar to the standard tooth blades, but with every other tooth missing. The space between teeth is much wider and the design provides for fast sawdust removal and cool and smooth cuts.

Double tooth blades

This is a skip tooth blade with a large space between sets of two teeth. They cut slightly slower, but leave a very smooth cut.

Reverse tooth blades & ultra reverse tooth blades

They are exactly like the regular skip tooth blade, except that the last few bottom teeth point upward. This prevents tear-out or splintering on the bottom of the cut and is especially good to use with plywood.

Precision ground blades

This is a skip tooth blade with small teeth that have been ground to shape, rather than simply filed. They are much sharper and unlike any other blades, cut in a straight line. They last longer and leave a very smooth surface. These are very aggressive blades and are quite expensive.

Spiral tooth blades

These are either a group of blades twisted together or a regular flat blade that is twisted before it is hardened. There are teeth all the way around the blade and you can cut in all directions without turning the wood. They generally leave a rough surface and wide kerfs, cannot make a tight or sharp corner, and have a tendency to stretch with use.

Crown tooth blades

The teeth on these blades are shaped like a crown with a space between each of them. There is no upside down with these blades, so they can be put in either way. They cut a little slower than a regular blade, but are good for cutting plastic and acrylic.

~~~~~

My blades of choice are the Flying Dutchman™ reverse tooth blades for their quality and the smooth cuts they produce. The reverse teeth at the bottom end of the blade eliminates burrs at the back of hardwood and tear-outs at the back of ply wood, reducing the amount of hand sanding required after cutting. A standard blade with no reverse teeth cuts faster and more aggressively than the reverse tooth blade, but will leave burrs at the back of the cut that will have to be removed with sandpaper.

1.6 Drilling Blade Entry Holes

Drill blade entry holes through the work piece in the areas indicated on the pattern.

Use a hand drill if you do not have access to a drill press.

Remove burs created by drilling the holes with a scraper blade along the grain of the workpiece at a slight angle or use sandpaper.

Most projects require making inside cuts. Simply drill small holes through the work piece in the areas indicated on the pattern. Thread the blade through the hole in the work piece and reattach it to the saw. A drill press, a hand drill, or a rotary tool can be used. For stack cutting, the blade entry holes should be drilled at a 90-degree angle into the stack and the best way to achieve this is by using a drill press. Use the smallest drill bit practically possible when drilling the holes for small areas in a design. Drill a little bit at a time and lift the bit out of the hole frequently to expel the waste. In a large waste area, it is best to drill the starter hole close to a corner rather than in the middle, as it will take less time for the blade to reach the pattern line. Always use a piece of scrap wood underneath the work piece to drill into. This prevents tear out at the bottom of the project.

For some projects, one needs to drill very small holes in thicker material like 3/4" or 1" wood or MDF. This can present the problem of drill bits breaking easily or veering off to one side in wood with hard and soft variations in the grain. A tiny bit generates a lot of heat in thick wood, causing them to become brittle after some use. Here are a few things to try:

• Buy good quality high-speed steel (HSS) bits.
These are more resistant to the effect of heat, especially when drilling in hardwood. Other options are tungsten carbide tipped or titanium tipped bits, but they are quite expensive compared to HSS bits
• Spot the planned holes prior to drilling by tapping them with a center punch
• Use a high speed and a 'nibble' action.
Back out repeatedly to clear the bit's flutes of wood shavings.
• Hold the wood down firmly but gently, with just enough force to keep it from lifting from the table.
• Let the bit do the work; do not apply any force.

BE sure to remove burrs created by drilling the holes. If the burrs are not removed, your work piece will not be flush on the saw table and this will prevent it from moving easily on the table during cutting.

1.7 Making Cuts

Cutting absolutely straight lines on the scroll saw requires some practice.

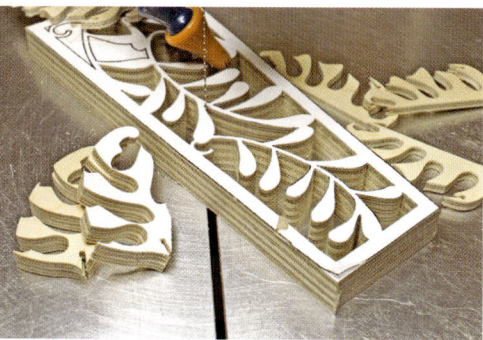

Try to cut directly on the line, as cutting too far to one side of the line may spoil the design's integrity.

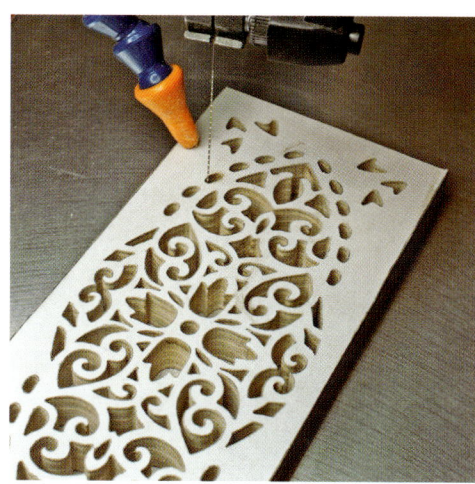

The blade you use will be dictated by the wood thickness, amount of cutting detail, and sharp radius turns required. Do not attempt to get extra use from a dull blade. Immediately change to a new blade at the first sign of charring in the cut or when you start having difficulty keeping to the pattern line. Dull blades tend to wander from the line of cut and make inclined cuts that are not vertical. Avoid backing up and re-cutting an inside line if you happen to wander away from the line of cut, as this causes untidy cutting results. Allow the blade to do the cutting. Do not apply too much feeding pressure by forcing the wood into the blade.

Making some preliminary practice cuts is recommended until confidence is gained and various lines can be followed consistently. Cutting absolutely straight lines or perfectly round circles on the scroll saw requires some practice. Patience and practice are the keys to developing sawing skills. For most projects the pattern provides thin cutting lines to follow. Try to cut directly on the line. Cutting too far to one side of the line may spoil the integrity of the design.

If you are right handed, you will be more comfortable cutting with the largest portion of the work pieces to the right of your blade. Left-handed scrollers should work with the largest part of the work piece on the left side of the blade. Hand position is the most critical aspect of controlling your work piece. Do not put your hands at the edge of your work piece. Position them about an inch away from either side of the blade to control the wood movement. Keep your fingers away from the front of the scroll saw blade. All you need is a light touch to hold the wood; a white-knuckled hold only tires you out and makes the wood more difficult to turn. Thick wood needs to be held down much more firmly than thin wood.

Think ahead. When you approach a sharp turn in the pattern, reposition your hands in preparation. Unless you are sawing in a straight line, your hands should be constantly

Position your hands about an inch away from either side of the blade to control the wood movement.

moving around the wood to better position yourself for the turns. Watch your hand movements. If you find yourself turning your body to control the movements of the work piece, stop and reposition yourself. Always stand or sit directly in front of the machine for best control.

It is imperative to keep the blade moving when attempting to turn your work piece. At first you will have a tendency to stop the motor when going into a tight turn. This causes the wood to pick up and smash back down on the table. Keep the motor going, and listen to your machine. You should not hear any sawing noise when you make a 90-degree turn. Make the turn by putting your finger fairly close to the blade to allow the wood piece to pivot around the blade.

When you cut out a circle, keep the feeding speed constant. If you continually stop and start as you make the turn, the finished edge will be choppy.

Cutting Delicate Areas

Slow down the speed of your saw when cutting thin material or fragile parts in the pattern.

I am often asked what the secret is to making delicate fretwork cuts where the bridge between two openings is very small or where there are small delicate protrusions in the design. It can be very frustrating to spend hours scrolling a project, only to have it spoiled because you break a piece of the design. There are several things you can do to increase your chances of successfully scrolling these areas, and hopefully these tips will prove helpful to you.

First, let's assume you're using 1/8" or 1/4" plywood. It is very important to use good quality plywood, such as Baltic birch. Buy the best grade ply available to reduce the risk of splintering, chipping, and breakage. Pre-sand the wood to minimize the amount of hand sanding to be done after cutting, thereby reducing the risk of breaking fragile pieces during sanding.

I strongly recommend stack cutting extra layers of wood. Stacking the work pieces allows for more controlled cutting of thin material. Also, if a piece happens to break during cutting or sanding, you will have an extra one available to use. Cutting is made much easier by stacking at least two layers of 1/8" thick wood. You may also want to consider adding a waste piece of material to the bottom of the stack. Because most of the burrs from cutting occur on the bottom layer, much less sanding will be required if that is a waste layer.

Joining the layers of wood for stack cutting can be done in different ways as described in *Chapter 1.2* for material preparation.

Use the smallest-size blade possible to cut the thickness of wood being used. The smaller the blade size, the less aggressively it cuts. Although reverse blades tend to lift the work piece on the up stroke, it is not very pronounced on small sized blades. I prefer to use the reverse blade because their cutting action results in fewer burrs left on the back of the project, thereby reducing the amount of sanding needed to be done afterwards. Change the blade regularly. Do not attempt to get extra use from a dull blade when cutting delicate areas. Not only does a dull blade not provide a clean cut, but it can also break at a critical stage of cutting, causing breakage of fragile pieces.

Many projects have been broken due to a lack of concentration...whatever you do, don't drop it! Of course, if the worst happens and you do happen to break a project with delicate pieces, it can sometimes be fixed with the help of quick drying wood glue. First, be sure to retrieve the correct pieces from the waste. Test the salvaged pieces in the project to guarantee they fit well. Squeeze some glue onto a piece of scrap wood, and use a toothpick to apply glue to the joining surfaces. Squeeze the pieces together and remove the glue squeeze-out using a clean cloth. Leave the project on a level surface while the glue dries.

Before cutting, it is important that the blade entry holes be drilled at a 90° angle into the stack; the best way to achieve this is by using a drill press. Use the smallest drill bit possible when drilling the holes for the small areas. Drill a little bit at a time, and frequently lift the drill bit out of the hole to expel the waste.

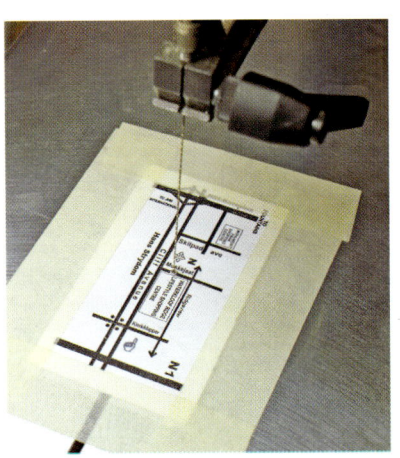

A zero clearance insert is a good way to keep the work pieces stable while cutting fragile areas. These inserts, generally made of plastic, are available for certain scroll saw brands. Alternatively, you can make your own disposable zero clearance insert using a piece of carton or a business card. Drill a tiny hole in the center of the piece, and secure it to the saw table using four strips of clear packing tape or masking tape. Thread the blade through the drilled hole. As you progress with the project, the blade will enlarge the hole to the point where you need to replace the insert with a new one.

A MORE permanent alternative is to use a piece of plywood about the size of the saw table. Use a fine blade and make a straight cut to the center of the wood, then pivot the wood around the blade to make a small hole for the blade to come through when you cut your projects. Attach the wood to the saw table with double-sided tape.

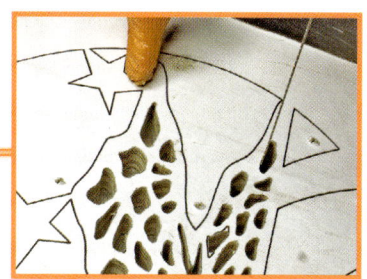

WHEN you get to the end of a cut, do not allow the blade to expel the waste piece. The force by which the waste piece is ejected from the opening can easily cause breakage of delicate pieces of the design. Instead, stop the saw just as you get to the end of the cut, and carefully remove the waste piece. A spare blade works well for pushing the waste piece out of the opening.

Slow down the speed of your saw for more controlled cutting, especially when cutting tiny curves and circular shapes. When you encounter two cut lines in the pattern that are close together, keep to the outside of the lines. This way, the chance of ruining the project is reduced if the blade should veer off the line at a critical part of the design.

When cutting delicate areas in a design, stacking the work pieces allows for more controlled cutting of thin material.

To provide stability for the fragile areas while you are cutting, replace the waste cut outs into the work piece, and secure them using clear tape at the top and bottom of the stack. If you prefer not to replace the waste pieces and did not use a disposable layer on the bottom of the stack, another good practice is to sand the burrs on the back of the stack at regular intervals, while there is still more stability in the work piece and fewer delicate pieces to catch and break.

Take care when prying apart the layers of the stack. I insert a scraper blade between the layers to separate them as pulling the layers apart by force may cause breakage. Be sure to first loosen all the areas where double-sided tape was applied. Any glue residue from the double-sided tape can be removed using mineral spirit or surgical spirit after the pieces are separated.

From my experience, most breakage of delicate pieces does not actually occur during cutting, but while sanding them. Make sure you have a sturdy, level surface available for sanding projects. Do not attempt to sand fragile pieces while holding the project in one hand; it is best done secured on a flat surface. Use small pieces of sandpaper, and sand by hand rather than using a sanding block. You will have a better feel as to the amount of pressure required when sanding in this way. Hold the work piece firmly on the work surface with one hand while sanding with the other.

1.8 Assembling & Finishing the Project

Sanding

If the project is going to be displayed, it is sure to collect dust. Cleaning is easier if there is a finish on the project. A finish protects the project, some more than others. It also allows the natural color and grain of the wood to emerge and enhances the beauty of the wood.

Proper preparation is necessary before applying a finish. Pre-sanding the wood before cutting minimizes the amount of sanding to be done later. Once the work pieces are complete, hand sanding is normally the method used. For flat projects without too many fragile cuts, a palm sander or random orbital sander can be used. To remove the burrs, lightly sand the back of the project using a sanding mop or a flap sander. To clean up fret cuts and ridges where the cuts meet, try emery boards cut down to serve as sanding sticks, small needle files, or stiff cloth-backed sanding paper cut to small strips. Sometimes sanding paper wrapped around a piece of dowel stick or toothpick can be handy. Hand sanding grips in various shapes, angles, and profiles are available. These are useful for sanding larger convex and concave areas as well as curves and corners.

A disc sander is a handy tool for sanding perfect circles and to sand straight edges of work pieces.

When sanding wood, you can only sand it as smooth as the pores will allow. A stage is reached where you cannot get the wood any smoother irrespective of the grade of sandpaper you use. It may feel smoother, but what is happening is that the fine dust is filling the pores and grain and when you remove this dust prior to applying a finish, the timber will return to its smoothest attainable state.

Always sand with the grain and start with the roughest paper/smallest number necessary, depending on the amount of sanding required. Work through the various grits towards the smoothest paper/largest number. Sandpaper ranges from 50-grit or 80-grit, which is very rough, to 600-grit or 800-grit, which is very smooth. Remove the dust from the project between grit changes. Use a hard bristled paintbrush or an air compressor nozzle.

Use a router with a cove bit or a round over bit to create decorative edges to work pieces.

Assembling

1. Work on a sturdy level surface for gluing. Dry fit the work pieces first and sand or cut them as needed for a good fit.

2. Apply wood glue to the meeting surfaces and join the work pieces together. To glue an overlay to a project, small beads of glue are applied to the back of the overlay piece.

3. Strips of masking tape are handy to keep the pieces in place while you line them up.

4. Apply clamps or large rubber bands and remove any excess glue using a clean damp cloth. A toothpick can also be used to remove small amounts of glue squeeze-out. Put the project aside for the glue to dry. If needed, scrape away any glue residue using a scraper blade and re-sand these areas.

Varnishes

Varnish is a reactive finish in that it dries by chemical reaction. Lacquer and shellac are evaporative finishes that dry by the evaporation of the solvent. There are different types of varnishes such as alkyd, polyurethane, and spar. An alkyd is very slow drying, has a warm color and a moderately hard finish. Polyurethane is faster drying, provides a harder finish, and the color is not as warm as for alkyd. Spar is used for outdoor projects, has a softer finish, is slow drying, and has an amber color. Then there are also water-based varnish and gel varnish. The choice of finish will depend on the appearance you want to achieve and the durability required. When you are using a varnish for the first time, test it on a piece of scrap wood first.

Many kinds of spray varnishes and clear lacquers are available and choices include gloss, semi gloss, and satin finishes. When applying the first coat of some finishes, a raise of the grain (also known as the bloom) occurs in varying amounts, depending on the product and the wood. Once dry, the first coat must be sanded down to remove the bloom. Use 280-grit to 320-grit sandpaper and sand with the grain. Light coats of finish give better results than heavy coats. Sand the surfaces between coats with 280- to 320-grit sandpaper.

For liquid varnishes, read and follow the manufacturer's instructions. Sand the project between layers and remove the sanding dust with a soft brush, slightly damp cloth, or compressed air before applying the next coat. Generally three coats are required but for open grained wood like oak, more coats may be needed to fill the grain for a smooth finish.

> **Tip**
>
> THE next step is not necessary if you use a liquid varnish that is painted on the wood. You may also skip this process, if you prefer, for projects made of plywood. If you use a wood stain on the project, first allow the stain to dry thoroughly. Skip the steps for the oil or wax liquid and apply either spray varnish or a liquid varnish.

Apply Danish oil™, Tung oil, lemon oil, or boiled linseed oil to the project, following the manufacturer's directions. I prefer to use a deep penetrating furniture wax liquid instead, as it dries much quicker than oil. Use a small sized artist's brush to reach the surfaces of delicate inside cuts. A paintbrush is used for larger projects. If the project is small, it can be dipped in the finish. Wipe off the excess using a lint free cloth (an old t-shirt works well) and allow it to dry. Place the project in the sun if possible. This process allows the grain and color to emerge and removes fine dust trapped in the grain of the wood. The drying period depends on the type of wood you are using, the particular finish you applied, and the weather condition. Once the oil or wax liquid is completely absorbed and dry, the project is ready for spray varnishing.

For spray varnishes, wear a mask to protect yourself from the fumes. Spray in a well ventilated area. I always do my spray varnishing outside in the sun, for quick drying. Make sure that the area is clean and dust free before you spray, as you do not want small dust particles adhering to your finish. One way to achieve a dust free environment is to use a large cardboard box on its side as a spray booth, with the project placed on a brick inside the box.

You might prefer a liquid varnish instead of a spray varnish. The drying time for these finishes is a lot longer and cannot be rushed. They are applied with a brush and there are various types available.

Adding/Changing Color

There is nothing nicer than the grain and pattern of a beautiful piece of hardwood. However, sometimes we work with less attractive wood or we need to change the color of a piece of hardwood for a particular reason. Some projects also benefit from having some color added. Here are various options for staining or coloring wood and tips for their application.

Wood Stain

Mix stains to make your own colors. Mixing a dark stain like walnut with a lighter one like light oak will provide you with a nice medium brown color.

If the color is too intense for your purpose, then keep a rag handy and be sure to wipe away the stain as soon as you have applied it. You can also rub away the stain after application by wiping it with the rag dipped in lacquer thinners. For a less intensive color, dilute the stain with some lacquer thinners first.

Always test the stain on a piece of scrap of the same wood you are using for the project. Allow each coat to dry thoroughly before applying a second coat. Work fast to reduce streaking and lines.

It is preferable to wear gloves for staining wood, unless you don't mind having stained fingertips and nails for a few days.

Wood stain does not lift the grain and can be finished with several coats of clear spray lacquer or clear liquid varnish.

To quickly cover all the surfaces of smaller projects with detailed fret cuts, pour some stain in a foil baking dish and dip the project in the stain.

Acrylic Paints

Dilute the paint with water for the wood grain to be visible. If you are going to keep the diluted paint to use again later, use distilled water.

To make sure you get the effect you are after, test the color first on a piece of scrap of the same wood you are using for the project. Blue, for instance, applied to a yellow shade of wood will not be pure blue, but will have a green tinge.

Use several coats for more intensive color.

You can also paint the wood with undiluted paint and wipe it off while it is still wet. Use a rag or paper towel. If you are using wood with pronounced grain, this method will allow the paint to stay behind in the grain. An example of this technique would be to paint on and wipe away white acrylic on oak hardwood.

Mix acrylic paint with a water based liquid varnish for color and a finish in one. Several coats of this mixture may be needed to get a good finish.

To obtain an even paint finish on open grained wood, use a sealer or water based varnish first to prevent the paint from penetrating the wood. This also works if you want to add detail on the wood with a permanent marker, as it will prevent the marker ink from seeping into the grain.

The water-based paint will raise the grain, more so if a lot of water is used to dilute the paint. Sand between coats with 320-grit or 500-grit sandpaper, depending on the amount of raised grain.

You can also rub the surface of the wood with a piece of crumpled brown paper bag to smooth down the grain.

Once completely dry, either water based varnish or clear spray lacquer can be used as a finish.

FOR a combination of natural wood and paint, prepare your work piece and paint the surface with two even coats of a bright color, sanding in between coats. Once dry, apply several coats of clear spray varnish and let it dry. Cover the painted and varnished surface using masking tape or painters tape and apply a pattern with some fret cuts. Drill the holes, make the cuts, and remove the pattern and tape. The cut surfaces are natural wood while the face is colored. This technique provides a tidy end result that would be difficult to achieve if you paint the face surface after making the cuts.

Spray paints

MDF, plywood, and hardwoods can be spray-painted. Sand the wood to a smooth finish and remove the dust. MDF generally does not require much sanding. Wear a mask to protect yourself from the spray fumes, and spray in a well-ventilated area. If possible, do the spray painting outside in the sun for quick drying. As for spray varnishing, the area must be clean and dust free so that no small dust particles will adhere to the paint. Spread newsprint on the work area surface and use a brick or a block of wood to place your project on. As you spray, the brick can be turned around so that the back surface of the project is reached. Another option is to use a lazy Susan for easy spray painting of all surfaces. You may also want to consider using a large cardboard box on its side as a spray booth, with the project elevated on a brick inside the box.

One or two base coats of mat black or mat white paint may be applied. Mat white is sometimes referred to as appliance white. The mat paint provides better coverage than gloss paint, especially on the inside surfaces of fret cuts. Once the base coats are dry, apply several light coats of the color you have chosen for your project. Always allow each coat to dry thoroughly before applying the next and sand the surfaces between coats with 500-grit to 800-grit sandpaper. Light coats of paint give much better results than heavy coats.

Some interesting effects can be achieved by mixing spray paint colors. A second color can be applied lightly while the first coat is still wet. A contrasting color can be spattered on to the wet paint of the first coat.

Detail can be painted on a project with a fine tipped artist's brush. Apply a spurt of paint in a concentrated area on a sheet of paper and dip the brush in the paint. Work quickly as the paint will dry fast. This method can also be used to dip an old toothbrush in spray paint for applying spatters to the project. As soon as you are finished, clean the brush with paint thinner.

Hardwood or plywood can be lightly sprayed with several thin coats of mat white spray paint, as I have done for the fairy luminary in *Chapter 2.2*. Medium rough sandpaper (such as 120-grit) is used to sand away the paint in places. The bare areas are sanded smooth using 220-grit and then 320-grit sandpaper before clear spray varnish is applied to seal the project. This method results in a weathered appearance and is also attractive when darker paint colors are used.

Always experiment first on scrap wood of the same kind as you are using for the project. However, if you're not satisfied with a particular paint effect, just sand the surface and apply a few more coats of the required color. Spray-painted projects do not require a spray varnish finish.

Other finishing methods to consider are food coloring, leather dyes, rub on pastes, and even shoe polish. Experiment on scrap wood first!

Some components such as turn buttons, saw tooth hangers, hooks, and lamp kits are only fitted to the project after the finish has been applied. If acrylic is combined with a wood project, the acrylic pieces are glued to the lamp or nightlight after finishing.

An interesting contrast effect can be obtained in a luminary box project by spraying a different color on the inside surface of the box.

Create a weathered appearance by sanding away the paint in places.

Acrylic pieces are glued to the night light after the finish has been applied to the project.

1.9 Lighting Options

There are different lighting options available and you might have other preferences to the ones I suggest. They include battery operated torch light holders and globes, table lamp fittings, touch lights, strings of fairy lights, a variety of battery-operated candles, and wax candles in votive holders.

Complete lamp kits are available from certain suppliers, but the parts can also be bought separately. Hollow tube in various materials, diameters, and finishes can be purchased in a standard length and cut to the required size on the scroll saw. Use a fine-toothed metal cutting blade for this purpose.

With the use of Christmas lights, there are some safety precautions to follow:

- Test the lights before installation and inspect them for excessive kinking or wear, frayed wires, gaps in insulation, bare spots, and cracked or broken sockets. Sets that show signs of melting around bulbs are early indications of defective or incorrect lamps and these sets should not be used.
- When replacing miniature bulbs, be sure to use bulbs of the same voltage rating. Use, for example, a 3-volt lamp to replace a 3-volt lamp, or a 12-volt lamp to replace a 12-volt lamp. This is particularly important to prevent dangerous overheating, melting, and possible fire.
- Remember, bulbs are not marked individually with a voltage rating, so save the voltage information on the bulb packaging.
- Burned out bulbs should be replaced promptly because the remaining bulbs burn brighter and hotter for each burned out bulb.
- Mini lights should not be left on when unattended.

Some of the different lighting options that can be used for the projects. Included are wax candles, votives, LED tea lights, an LED wax candle, and fairy lights.

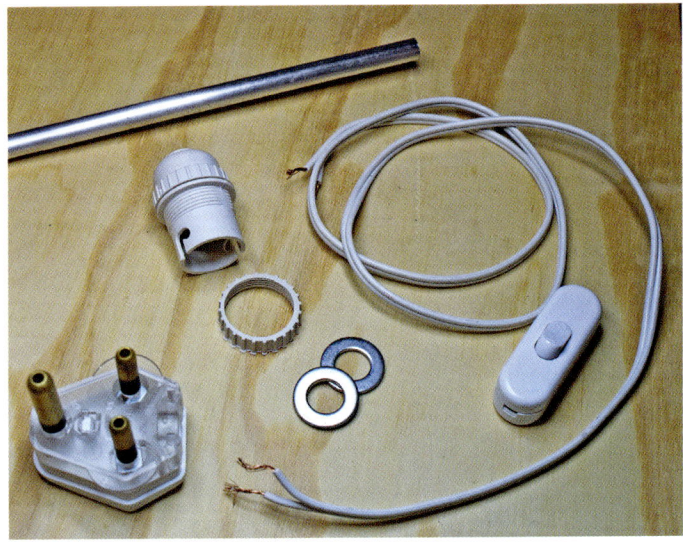

The basic parts required for a table lamp.

A strand of Christmas lights powered by a 9V battery.

Chapter 2

Luminaries

2.1 Tall Luminary

2.2 Fairy Luminary

2.3 Assorted Luminaries

2.4 Acrylic Luminary

2.5 Square Paper Luminary

2.6 Round Paper Luminaries

Traditionally luminaries are candles placed inside paper bags filled with sand. Wood luminaries are box structures consisting of five work pieces and can be cut from hardwood, plywood, or MDF. Acrylic can be used as an alternative material for making the box style luminaries.

It's not always easy to cut perfectly straight lines on the scroll saw. If you have access to a table saw, that can be used to cut the work pieces to the exact dimensions. I like using a disc sander to sand the edges of the box work pieces up to the pattern lines.

The boxes are assembled with all the work pieces joined to the outside of the base. The front and back pieces overlap the sides. Work on a sturdy level surface to do the glue-up procedure. Dry fit the work pieces first and sand or cut them as needed for a good fit. Apply small beads of glue to the joining surfaces and carefully bring the work pieces together. Strips of masking tape are handy to keep the pieces in place while you line them up. Apply clamps or large rubber bands and remove any excess glue using a clean damp cloth. Put the boxes aside so that the glue can dry.

If you are applying wood stain, it is best done after assembly. First scrape away any glue residue using a scraper blade and re-sand these areas.

Luminaries made of MDF are painted using acrylic paints or spray paints. Use one color for the project or paint a different color on the inside surface for an interesting contrast.

Tea light candles can be used with the wood and acrylic luminaries provided basic safety rules for candles are observed. These include not placing them in a draft and never leaving burning candles unattended. Candles are not to be used as nightlights. Battery operated tea lights and votives are a safe and easy alternative to use in your luminaries. Various shapes and sizes are available.

The numerous inside openings of the tall luminary creates a dazzling effect when illuminated.

2.1 Tall Luminary

The numerous inside openings of this pattern provide a design that resembles lace and the end result is well worth the effort. My project is crafted from 1/4" marine ply, with walnut wood stain used to create a dark colored finish. This luminary will also be attractive constructed from a dark colored hardwood like walnut, mahogany, or teak. If preferred, the fret design may be omitted from the side panels. The base may be substituted for a larger platform of thicker wood with a decorative routed edge.

Using a disc sander, sand the edges of the work pieces up to the perimeter pattern lines.

Pour wood stain into a foil baking dish and dip the completed project in the stain to cover all the surfaces.

After drilling the blade entry holes, use a scraper blade to remove burrs from the back of the work piece.

Tall luminary, base. Cut 1 from 1/4" material.

Two work pieces are stacked together for making the fret cuts of the side panels.

Patterns

Tall luminary, front. Cut 1 from 1/4" material. Use the outline to cut a solid matching back.

Tall luminary, side. Cut 2 from 1/4" material.

2.2 Fairy Luminary

The fairy design has some fragile fretwork cuts in parts of the pattern where the bridge between two openings is quite small and where there are small delicate protrusions. Refer to the "Basics" section in *Chapter One* for tips on making these cuts. The project is made of 1/4" plywood that is painted with several thin coats of white spray paint. Medium-rough sandpaper such as 120-grit is used to sand away the paint in places. The bare areas are sanded smooth using 220-grit and then 320-grit sandpaper, before clear spray varnish is applied to seal the project. This method results in a weathered appearance and is also attractive when darker paint colors are used. Always experiment first on scraps of the same kind of wood you are using.

Stack-cut the side work pieces.

Once the straight edges are sanded, and the inside openings are cut, the pattern and masking tape is removed.

For a weathered appearance, use medium-rough sandpaper such as 120-grit, to sand away the white paint in places.

Patterns

Fairy luminary, front. Cut 1 from 1/4" material. Use this outline to cut a matching solid back.

Fairy luminary, base.
Cut 1 from 1/4" material.

Fairy luminary, side.
Cut 2 from 1/4" material.

2.3 Assorted Luminaries

MDF or 1/4" plywood is required to make these luminaries of various themes. There are two sizes and the boxes can be stained, painted, or left natural. The bases and the back and side pieces can be stacked to save time and effort. Cut the stacks on the scroll saw or use a disc sander to sand the straight edges up to the pattern lines. Refer to the "Basics" section in *Chapter One* for tips on wood stacking, staining, and spray painting.

Make the fret cuts in the front pieces.

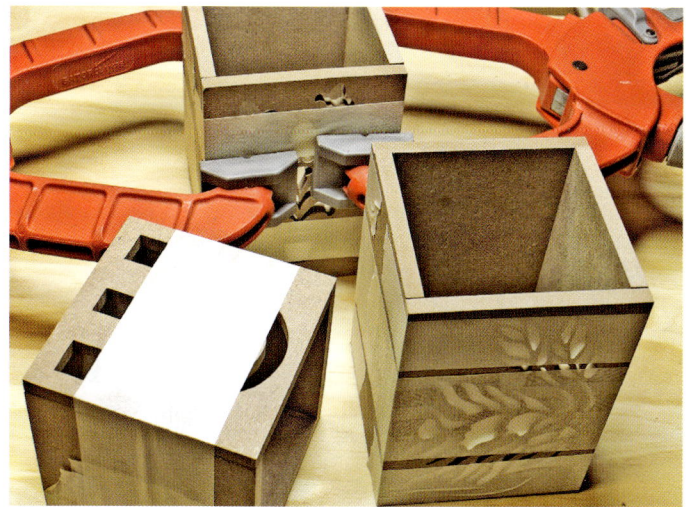

To glue up the boxes, use strips of masking tape to keep the work pieces in place while they are being lined up and clamped.

Wood stain is applied to the boxes using a large sized artist's brush.

Patterns

Assorted luminaries, side. Small size.
Cut 2 from 1/4" material.

Assorted luminaries, side. Medium size.
Cut 2 from 1/4" material.

Assorted luminaries, back. Medium size.
Cut 1 from 1/4" material.

Outer Shape: Assorted luminaries, back. Small size.
Cut 1 from 1/4" material.

Inner Shape: Assorted luminaries, base. Small or medium size.
Cut 1 from 1/4" material.

Christmas Bell Luminary, front. Medium size.
Cut 1 from 1/4" material.

Diamonds Luminary, front. Medium size.
Cut 1 from 1/4" material.

Hearts Luminary, front. Small size. Cut 1 from 1/4" material.

Religious Luminary, front. Small size. Cut 1 from 1/4" material.

Flower Luminary, front. Medium size.
Cut 1 from 1/4" material.

Halloween Luminary, front. Medium size.
Cut 1 from 1/4" material.

2.4 Acrylic Luminary

Use 1/4" acrylic for this project; acrylic can be stacked on top of scrap plywood. It can also be sandwiched between two layers of plywood. This method reduces the problem of the plastic melting due to heat generated by the friction of the blade. The result is a clean and smooth cut surface. Do not remove the protective masking film until you are ready to do the assembly.

Special adhesives are available for bonding the acrylic work pieces. Strips of masking tape are essential for keeping the pieces in place while you line them up. Apply clamps or large rubber bands and remove any excess adhesive using a clean damp cloth. The drying time for different acrylic adhesives vary and can be as long as twenty-four to forty-eight hours. Refer to the "Basics" section in *Chapter One* for tips on drilling, cutting, and gluing acrylics.

Thin double-sided tape is used to stack the two side work pieces.

Lay out the pieces on a flat surface for the assembly.

31

Patterns

Acrylic luminary, front. Cut 1 from 1/4" material. Cut a second solid piece for the back.

Acrylic luminary, side. Cut 2 from 1/4" material.

Acrylic luminary, base. Cut 1 from 1/4" material.

2.5 Square Paper Luminary

A combination of 1/8" plywood and textured heavyweight paper is used for these projects. Patterns are provided for box frames in two sizes. If you are working with Baltic birch plywood, choose paper in natural colors. For luminaries in bright colors, use MDF for the frames, apply spray paints, and select paper colors to match.

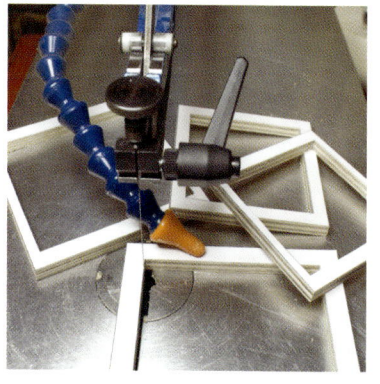

Cut the box frame pieces on the scroll saw.

A selection of textured heavyweight paper in natural colors.

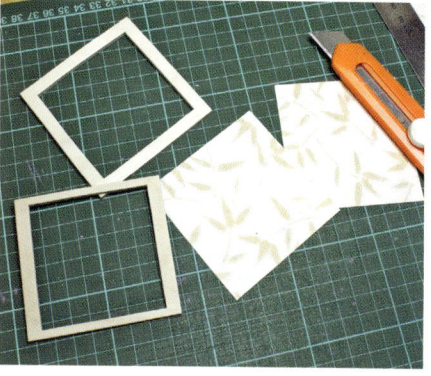

Use a blade cutter and ruler to cut pieces of paper to fit the frames.

Glue the paper to the inside surfaces of the box frames.

Attach strips of masking tape to the front and back pieces and lay out the box pieces on a flat surface.

Glue-up the box using wood glue.

Apply clamps to the box and allow the glue to dry.

Patterns

Square Paper Luminary, front and back. Large size. Cut 1 each from 1/8" material.

Square Paper Luminary, front and back. Small size. Cut 1 each from 1/8" material.

Outer shape:
Square Paper Luminary, side. Large size. Cut 2 from 1/8" material.

Inner shape:
Square Paper Luminary, side. Small size. Cut 2 from 1/8" material.

Outer shape:
Square Paper Luminary, base. Large size. Cut 1 from 1/8" material.

Inner shape:
Square Paper Luminary, base. Small size. Cut 1 from 1/8" material.

2.6 Round Paper Luminaries

1/4" hardwood, plywood or MDF is required for these simple round stands. Work pieces can be stacked to make several at the same time.

Stack cut the inner circle of the overlay piece. Separate the pieces and sand the inner surfaces by hand.

Attach the overlay work piece to the base using wood glue.

Cut the outer circle, or use a disc sander to sand up to the perimeter line, and finish the stand as preferred. Three small wooden balls can be glued to the bottom of the stand as feet.

Use a standard letter size sheet of textured heavyweight paper and use a blade cutter and ruler to cut horizontal strips. The height of the luminaries can vary, but my suggestion is to make them between 2 and 4 inches tall. Apply a narrow strip of thin double-sided tape to the inside edge of the paper strip.

YOU may want to construct your cylinders first and make sure that the inside circle of your stand matches in size before cutting those openings.

Important reminder: Do **not** use ordinary candles with paper luminaries. Use battery operated tea lights or votive candles.

Remove the backing from the tape and stick down the other end of the paper to make a cylinder shape. To secure the cylinder inside the stand, use small pieces of thin double-sided tape. Alternatively small beads of wood glue can be applied.

Patterns

Round Paper Luminary, overlay. Cut 1 from 1/4" material. Cut a second, solid circle for the base.

Chapter 3

Nightlights

3.1 Cherubs Nightlight

3.2 Fairy on Moon Nightlight

3.3 Pine Cones Nightlight

3.4 Bright Sun Nightlight

3.5 Decorative Fret Nightlight

By definition, a nightlight is a dim light that is kept burning throughout the night. A nightlight is equally attractive when used as a decorative accent on a table or shelf. For a dim light, use low wattage incandescent light bulbs or the low output LED light bulbs. Torch light holders and bulbs connected to a 9-volt battery is another option where a small size light fitting is required.

Using 1/4" hardwood or plywood for the boxes and 1" hardwood for the top pieces, form a decorative edge for the top piece using a router with a cove bit. Choose hardwood to match the color of the plywood used for the box. Alternatively apply wood stain to the box and top piece for a uniform color, as I have done for the Bright Sun Nightlight project. You may also use a top piece of contrasting color wood if preferred. For box work pieces with perfect straight edges, use a disc sander or belt sander and sand up to the pattern lines.

Measure the diameter of the lamp holder you will be using and adjust the size of the circle on the back pattern piece before you cut the opening. Aim for a snug fit where no glue is required. If the light fitting needs to be adhered into the opening in the back work piece; it is best done before the box is assembled. However, if the light holder fits securely in the opening without glue, it can be inserted after assembly.

With the exception of the detailed fret design light, the nightlights are simple box structures consisting of four or five work pieces. The boxes are assembled with all the work pieces joined to the outside of the base, and with the front and back pieces overlapping the sides. Work on a sturdy level surface to do the glue-up procedure. Dry fit the work pieces first and sand or cut them as needed for a good fit. Apply small beads of glue to the joining surfaces and carefully bring the work pieces together. Strips of masking tape are handy to keep the pieces in place while you line them up. Apply clamps or large rubber bands and remove any excess glue using a clean damp cloth. Put the boxes aside for the glue to dry.

Position the top piece in the center of the box and level with the back of the box. Secure using wood glue and apply large clamps, or place a heavy weight on top of the box assembly while the glue dries.

If you are applying wood stain to the projects, it is best done after assembly. First scrape away any glue residue using a scraper blade and re-sand these areas.

A piece of clear or frosted acrylic may be mounted on the inside of the fretwork to diffuse the light. Clear silicone or cyanoacrylate glue (CA glue or superglue™) is used for this purpose.

3.1 Cherubs Nightlight

Drill the blade entry holes for the fret design of the front piece.

This project can be made as an open light box, or with the option of adding a lid to reduce the amount of light that is emitted. I used marine plywood for my nightlight and applied light oak wood stain. Due to the larger size of this box, the lamp holder is glued in place after the box is assembled and the finish is applied.

Use 1/4" wood for the lid and 1/8" wood for the lid inner. To make the lid, cut the perimeter lines of the lid and lid inner patterns. Test-fit the lid inner in the box opening, it should just fall into the box. Center and glue the lid inner to the bottom surface of the lid.

A plastic lamp holder can be cut smaller to use for the project.

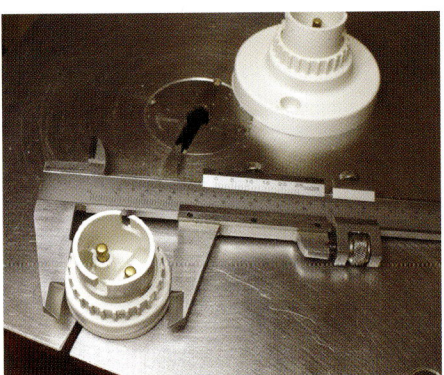

Measure the diameter of the light fitting and adjust the size of the opening on the back pattern piece accordingly. Use a compass to draw the circle for the opening.

Dry fit the work pieces before assembly and if needed sand or cut the pieces for a proper fit.

Glue up the box using wood glue.

Light oak wood stain is applied to the marine ply box.

Patterns

Cherubs nightlight, front. Cut 1 from 1/4" material. Use the outline to cut a solid back, adding a hole at the bottom center for electrical access (see inset).

Cherubs nightlight, back, showing location of hole for electrical access. Cut 1 from 1/4" material.

Cherubs nightlight, side. Cut 2 from 1/4" material.

Cherubs nightlight, base. Cut 1 from 1/4" material.

Outer shape:
Cherubs nightlight, lid. Cut 1 from 1/4" material.

Inner shape:
Cherubs nightlight, lid inner. Cut 1 from 1/8" material.

3.2 Fairy on Moon Nightlight

The fairy design has some fragile fretwork cuts in parts of the pattern. Refer to the "Basics" section in *Chapter One* for tips on making these cuts. I laminated two layers of 1/8" Baltic birch ply to obtain 1/4" material for this project. More information on laminating wood is available in the "Basics" section of *Chapter One*. After assembling my project, I decided to mount a piece of clear acrylic on the inside of the fairy design to diffuse the light. Clear silicone was used to secure the acrylic to the wood. Follow the manufacturer's directions. Normally silicone requires at least twelve hours drying time. The acrylic can also be glued to the front panel before the assembly is done.

Make the fret cuts of the fairy's wings before cutting the other inside openings.

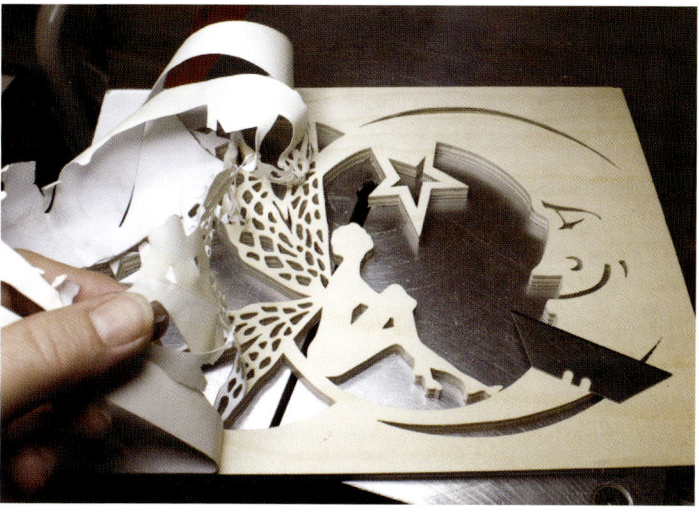

Once all of the inside cuts have been completed, remove the masking tape and pattern.

Using a sanding block or sand paper, remove the burrs at the back of the work piece at regular intervals.

Assemble the box with the front and back pieces overlapping the sides.

43

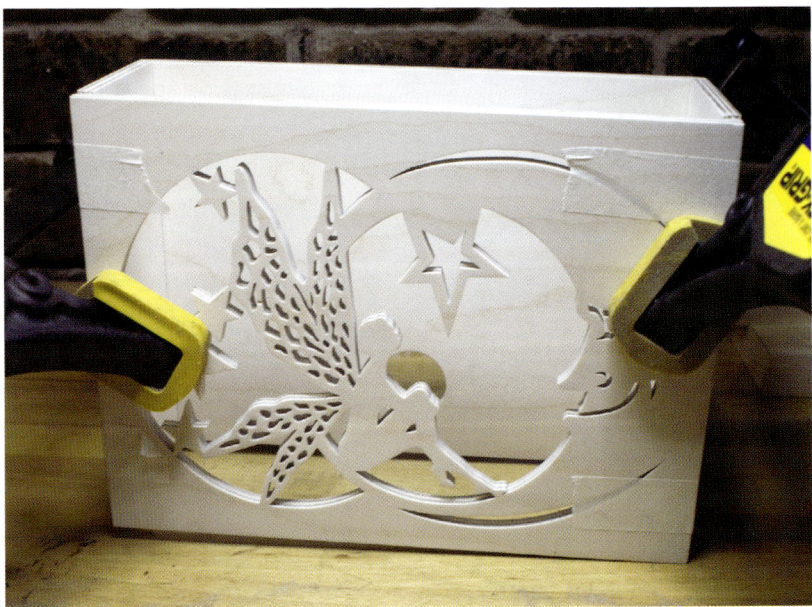

Apply wood glue to the connecting surfaces and assemble the box. Apply clamps and allow the glue to dry.

Apply clear silicone to the inside of the front panel.

Carefully insert the acrylic, apply clamps, and put the box aside to dry.

Patterns

Fairy on Moon nightlight, front. Cut 1 from 1/4" material. Use the outline to cut a solid back, adding a hole at the bottom center for electrical access (see inset).

Fairy on Moon nightlight, back, showing location of hole for electrical access. Cut 1 from 1/4" material.

Fairy on Moon nightlight, side.
Cut 2 from 1/4" material.

Fairy on Moon nightlight, top.
Cut 1 from 1" material.

3.3 Pine Cones Nightlight

Two layers of 1/8" Baltic birch ply was laminated to obtain 1/4" material for the pine cones nightlight. Refer to the "Basics" section in *Chapter One* for more information on laminating wood. I fitted a ceramic torch light holder for this project and used a hot glue gun with clear glue to fit the holder in the back opening. Epoxy glue can also be used.

While making the inside cuts, remove the burrs at the back of the work piece at regular intervals.

Secure the light holder in the back panel using a hot glue gun.

The light holder fits snugly in the back panel opening.

Patterns

Pine Cones nightlight, front. Cut 1 from 1/4" material. Use the outline to cut a solid back, adding a hole at the bottom center for electrical access (see inset).

Pine Cones nightlight, back, showing the location of the hole for electrical access. Cut 1 from 1/4" material.

Pine Cones nightlight, side. Cut 2 from 1/4" material.   Pine Cones nightlight, top. Cut 1 from 1" material.

3.4 Bright Sun Nightlight

This project is made from marine ply with blonde mahogany for the top piece. Water based cherry wood stain was used undiluted to achieve the bright reddish color. Light sanding with smooth grit sandpaper may be necessary after the stain has dried.

Carefully drill the blade entry holes of the openings in the front work piece pattern.

Thread the blade and cut the inside openings.

The straight edges for all the work pieces are sanded using the disc sander.

Cherry wood stain is applied to all the surfaces of the project with a large artist's brush.

The top piece is glued in place level with the back of the box.

Patterns

Bright Sun nightlight, front. Cut 1 from 1/4" material. Use the outline to cut a solid back, adding a hole at the bottom center for electrical access (see inset).

Bright Sun nightlight, back, showing location of hole for electrical access. Cut 1 from 1/4" material.

51

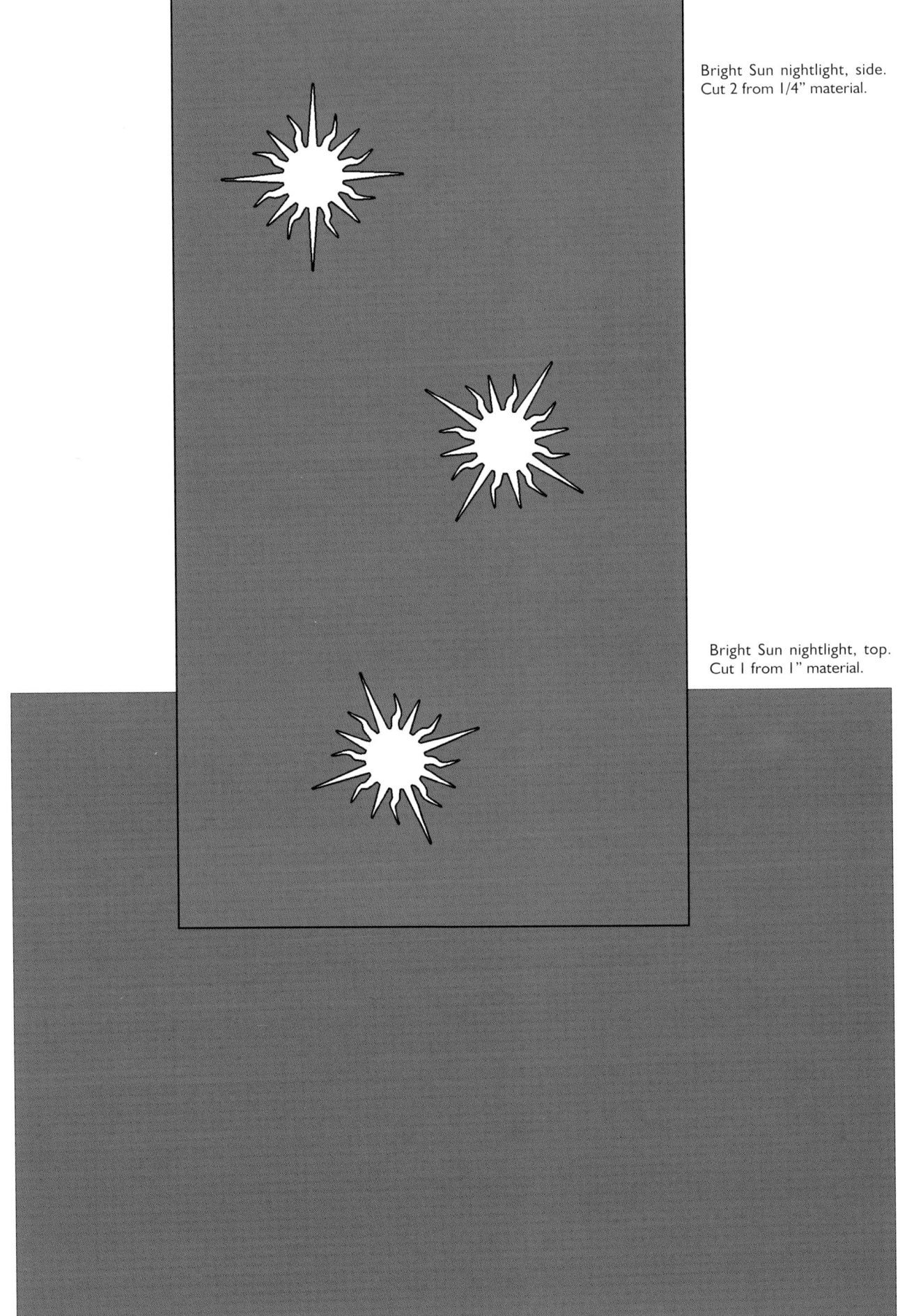

Bright Sun nightlight, side.
Cut 2 from 1/4" material.

Bright Sun nightlight, top.
Cut 1 from 1" material.

3.5 Decorative Fret Nightlight

This project with a detailed fret design has the tab and slot method for joining together the project pieces. Use 1/4" plywood or hardwood of choice. As an alternative, the project can also be made as a conventional table lamp by using a lamp kit.

To start, join together two layers of wood for each set of side panels and for the top and bottom pieces. Sand the straight edges of the work piece stacks using the disc sander. Drill blade entry holes and make the fret cuts first. Some of the openings are very tiny and will require a small size drill bit and blade.

Cut the slots and the perimeter lines of the side panels.

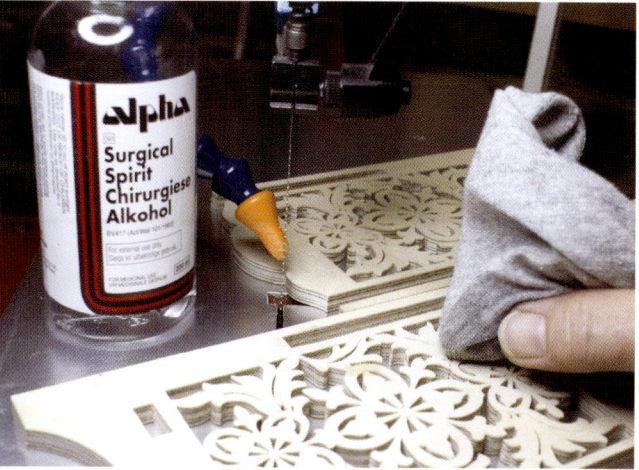

Remove the masking tape and patterns and separate the stacked layers of the side panels. Use mineral spirit or surgical spirit and a clean cloth to remove the sticky residue of the double-sided tape from the work pieces.

Cut the top and bottom pieces on the pattern lines.

Test fit the pieces.

The tabs of the top piece are inserted in the slots of two side panels. The tabs of the bottom piece are inserted in the slots of the other two side panels. Slide the slots of the top assembly over the slots of the bottom assembly. The pieces should fit neatly and tightly. To facilitate bulb changes when required, no glue will be used in the assembly. Make adjustments to the slots or tabs if needed.

53

Measure the diameter of the light fitting you have chosen and use a compass to draw the circle for the opening in the center of the bottom piece. Sand all the work pieces by hand and apply a finish of choice. Insert the light fitting in the bottom piece opening and secure it with glue that is appropriate for bonding the material of the selected fitting with the wood. Insert the bulb in the light fitting and reassemble the nightlight.

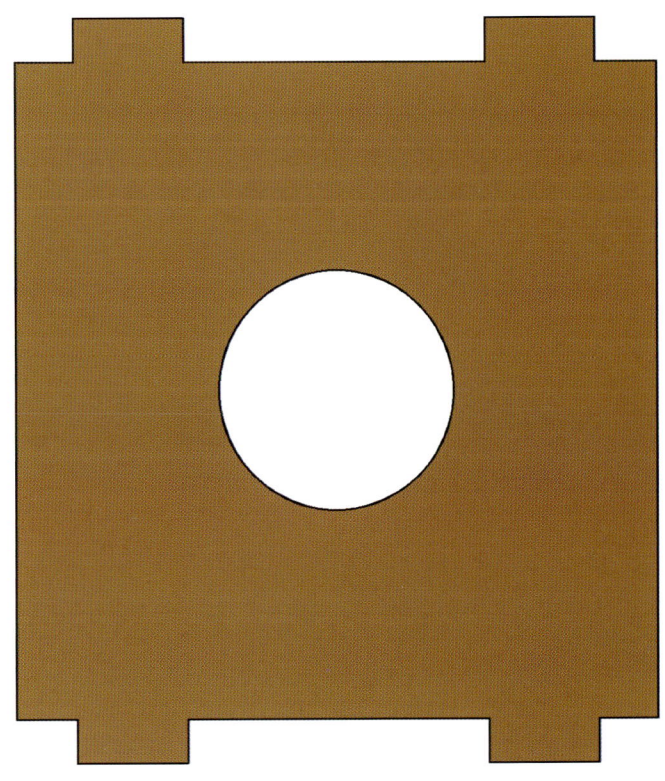

Decorative Fret nightlight, top and bottom. Cut 2 from 1/4" material.

Patterns

Decorative Fret nightlight, front and back with top slots.
Cut 2 from 1/4" material.

Decorative Fret nightlight, front and back with bottom slots.
Cut 2 from 1/4" material.

Chapter 4

Table Lamps

4.1 Lighthouse Lamp

4.2 Lamp with Overlays

A table lamp can be both decorative and functional and is generally used on a side table, bedside table, or desk. These projects have a central shaft for housing the electric cord and a lampshade is fitted to the top of the lamp holder.

Complete lamp kits are available from certain suppliers, but the parts can also be bought separately. Hollow tube in various materials, diameters, and finishes can be purchased in a standard length and cut to the required size on the scroll saw. Use a fine-toothed metal cutting blade for this purpose. For a dim light, use low wattage incandescent light bulbs or the low output LED light bulbs.

4.1 Lighthouse Lamp

This nautical theme lamp requires 2" wood for the lighthouse frame and 1/8" wood for the lighthouse overlays and the palm tree overlays. Use 1" wood for the base rim and 1/4" wood for the base. Wood of contrasting colors may be used. I chose to use light colored wood for the project and applied walnut wood stain to certain pieces. The lamp can also be made from MDF and painted with acrylics or spray paints in bright colors.

57

To make the hollow lamp base, apply the rim pattern to 1" wood and cut the inside line of the pattern and the opening for the electric cord.

Apply the base pattern to 1/4" wood and roughly cut the work piece approximately 1/8" beyond the pattern line. Drill the center hole for the cord-housing shaft. Adjust the size of the hole according to the diameter of the shaft you are using. Center the rim on the base and secure it with wood glue. Turn over the assembly and use the disc sander to sand the base up to the perimeter pattern line.

When constructing the lighthouse, cover the work pieces with masking tape. Use temporary bond spray adhesive or glue stick to apply the frame pattern to 2" wood and the overlay patterns to 1/8" wood.

Sand the straight edges at the bottom of the frame and the lighthouse overlays using the disc sander.

Use a center punch to mark the center point of both the top and bottom ends of the frame piece.

Drill holes on the marked positions on either end. These holes should be of a diameter to accommodate the shaft you are using. Drill a blade entry hole for the center portion of the frame piece.

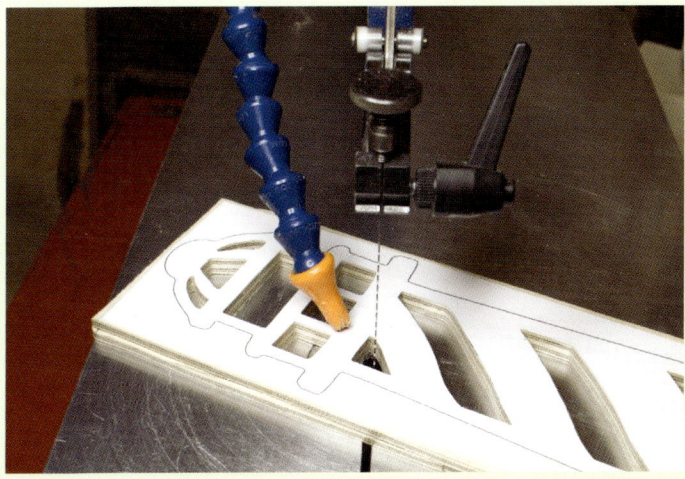

Cut the inner pattern line of the frame and the inside openings of the lighthouse overlays.

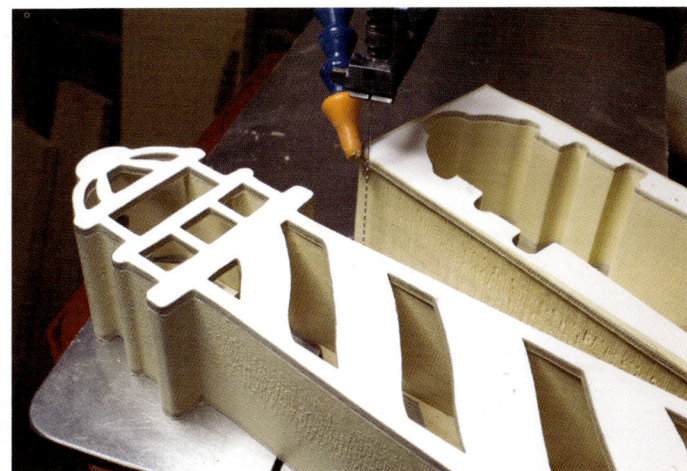

Line up the lighthouse overlays on the frame. Use small pieces of thin double-sided tape to attach the overlays on either side of the frame.

Cut the perimeter line of the lighthouse pattern through all three layers. Detach the work pieces.

59

Cut the palm trees overlay, and sand all the work pieces by hand.

Center the lighthouse assembly on the base and secure it with wood glue. Fit the lamp kit. The metal shaft with the electric cord is thread through the center holes of the project, and the lamp holder is fitted to the top of the shaft.

Apply a dark wood stain to the base, frame piece, and palm trees.

Use wood glue to attach the lighthouse overlays to the frame, apply clamps, and allow the glue to dry.

Attach palm trees to the front of the project using wood glue.

Patterns

Lighthouse table lamp, frame.
Cut 1 from 2" material.

Lighthouse table lamp, overlay.
Cut 2 from 1/8" material.

61

Lighthouse table lamp, base.
Cut 1 from 1/4" material.

Lighthouse table lamp, palm trees overlay. Cut 1 from 1/8" material.

Lighthouse table lamp, base rim. Cut 1 from 1" material.

4.2 Lamp with Overlays

The lamp structure is a box made from 1/4" wood and assembled with the front and back pieces overlapping the sides. Overlays are cut from 1/8" wood of contrasting color. Alternatively wood stain can be used to color the overlay pieces and frames. There are four different sets of overlay patterns to choose from in the patterns section. Hardwood with a thickness of 1" is used for the top and base of the lamp.

I used marine plywood for the box and MDF for the overlays. The box was stained a yellow brown color with light oak wood stain and walnut stain was applied to the overlays.

To begin, construct the box from the front, back, and side work pieces. The overlays and frames for each side of the lamp are cut from one piece of wood. Stack four layers of material so that all the overlays are cut at the same time

To finish, fit the lamp kit. The metal shaft with the electric cord is thread through the center holes of the project, and the lamp holder is fitted to the top of the shaft.

Sand the straight edges of the stack using the disc sander.

Drill the blade entry holes for the inside openings of the overlay stack and make the fret cuts of the overlay pieces.

Cut the perimeter lines of the overlays and the inside pattern line of the frame, and sand all the work pieces by hand.

Apply light oak wood stain to the box.

A medium sized artist's brush is used to apply walnut wood stain to the overlay frames.

The overlay pieces can be dipped in the stain.

Apply small beads of wood glue to the overlays and frames and glue them to the box sides.

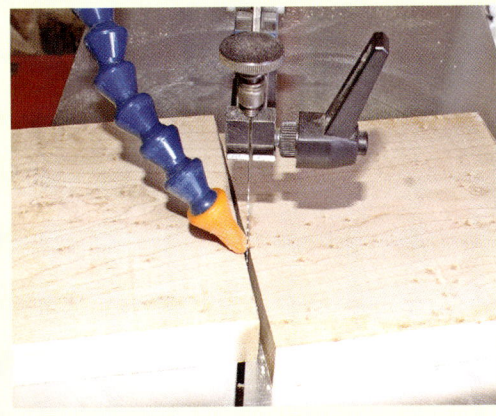

Cut the top and base pieces. Drill the center hole in each work piece for the cord-housing shaft. Adjust the size of the hole according to the diameter of the shaft you are using.

Use a router and a cove bit or a round over bit to create a decorative edge for the top and base pieces.

Apply deep penetrating furniture wax liquid or Danish oil™ to the top, base, and feet. *(Be sure to follow the manufacturer's directions.)*

Wooden balls or finials can be used as feet for the base.

Use a center punch to mark equal positions on the corners of the base and drill the holes for the finials.

Secure the feet to the base using wood glue.

Patterns

Table lamp with overlays, front and back.
Cut 1 each from 1/4" material.

Table lamp with overlays, side.
Cut 2 from 1/4" material.

Table lamp with overlays, frame and flowers overlay. Stack-cut 4 from 1/8" material.

Table lamp with overlays, frame and ducks overlay. Stack-cut 4 from 1/8" material.

Table lamp with overlays, frame and sea life overlay. Stack-cut 4 from 1/8" material.

Table lamp with overlays, frame and African design overlay. Stack-cut 4 from 1/8" material.

Table lamp with overlays, base and top. Cut 1 each from 1" material.

Chapter 5

Candle Stands and Sconce

With the exception of the patio candle lamp, wax candles can be used with these projects, provided basic safety rules for candles are observed. These include not placing them in a draft and never leaving burning candles unattended. Candles are not to be used as nightlights. Battery operated tea lights, votives, pillar candles, and taper candles are a safe and easy alternative.

5.1 Dolphin Votive Stand

5.2 Nativity Candle Stand

5.3 Cross Sconce

5.4 Compound-cut Candle Stand

5.5 Patio Candle Lamp

5.1 Dolphin Votive Stand

Here is a simple but attractive project made from 1" hardwood. A votive holder with a wire handle is hung from a hook in the dolphin's nose. The upright piece is secured into a slot cut in the base piece. My votive stand is made of light oak.

Apply the patterns to the two work pieces using your method of choice. Certain hardwoods like oak and cherry are prone to charring when they are cut. Cover the patterns with a layer of clear packing tape to assist in lubricating the blade, therefore reducing the chance of burning.

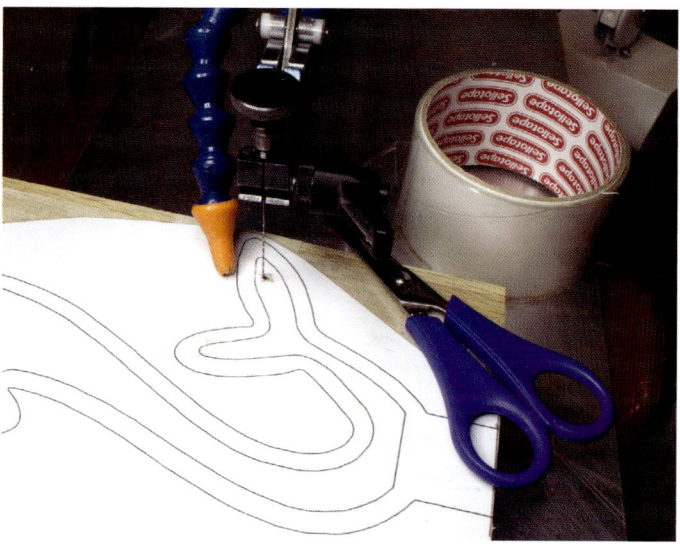

71

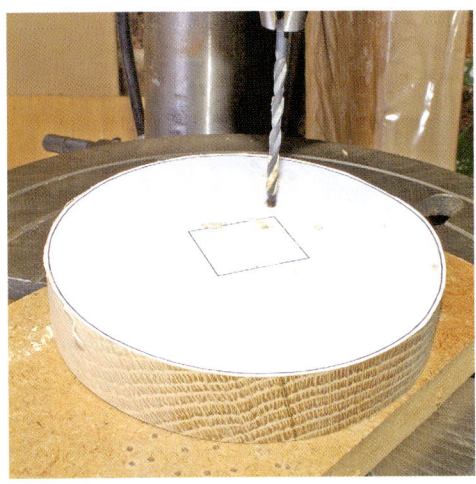

Drill the blade entry holes, and cut the inside pattern line of the dolphin and the slot in the base. Adjust the size of the slot opening according to the thickness of wood you are using.

Cut the perimeter line of the dolphin and the base. You may prefer to use a disc sander to sand the circular base up to the pattern line.

Drill a hole in the nose of the dolphin to accommodate a small threaded hook. Choose a drill bit diameter slightly smaller than that of the hook's thread.

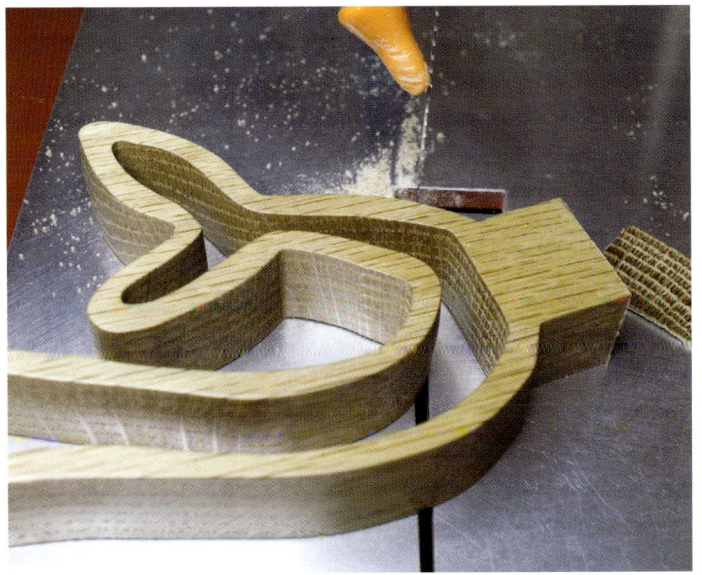

Sand the work pieces by hand, and apply deep penetrating furniture wax liquid or Danish oil™ to the pieces. *(Again, be sure to follow the manufacturer's directions.)*

Test fit the tab of the upright in the base slot. The tab should be level with the bottom of the base. If needed, cut the tab on the scroll saw for a proper fit. Use wood glue to secure the dolphin in the base and allow the glue to dry. Screw the hook in place.

Patterns

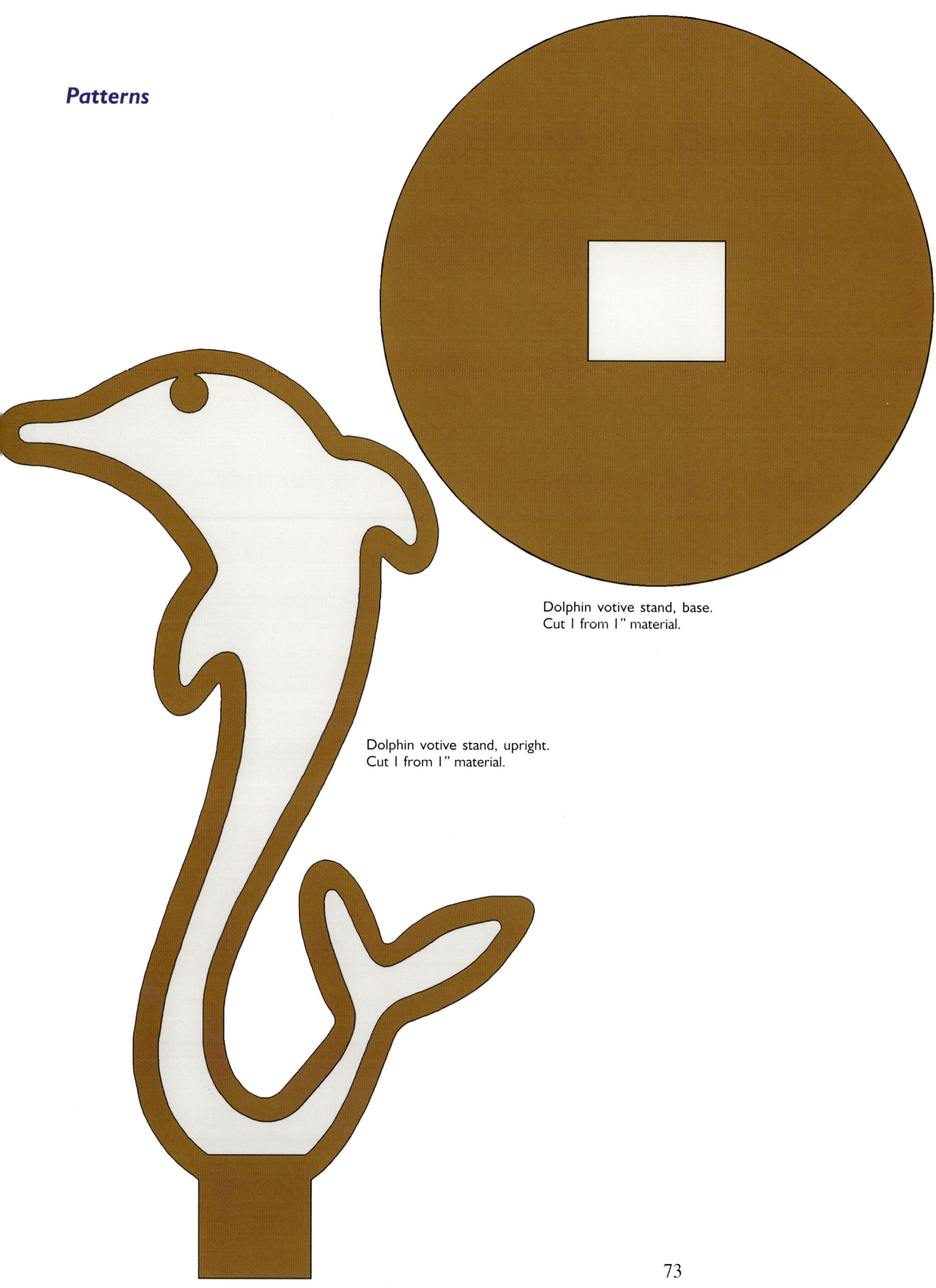

Dolphin votive stand, base.
Cut 1 from 1" material.

Dolphin votive stand, upright.
Cut 1 from 1" material.

5.2 Nativity Candle Stand

> **Tip**
>
> **OMIT** the candle cups and place a small display of wooden nativity figures and animals on the base. Use tea light candles or votives behind the upright to back light the fretwork.

This project consists of an upright and a base of 1/4" birch ply or wood of choice. The upright is inserted in a slot in the base. I laminated two layers of 1/8" Baltic birch ply to obtain 1/4" material for this project. More information on laminating wood is available in the "Basics" section of *Chapter One*. To make the stand in a different wood thickness, simply adjust the size of the base slot to accommodate the wood you are using.

The nativity design has some fragile fretwork cuts in parts of the pattern. Be careful not to catch and break these pieces during the sanding process.

Prepare the work piece to be cut to size.

Cut the slot and the perimeter pattern line of the base.

Apply deep penetrating furniture wax liquid or Danish oil™ to the work pieces, following the manufacturer's directions.

Use wood glue to attach two candle cups to the front part of the base.

Patterns

Nativity Candle Stand, upright. Cut 1 from 1/4" material.

Nativity Candle Stand, base.
Cut 1 from 1/4" material.

5.3 Cross Sconce

Blonde mahogany, also referred to as white lauan, was used for my cross sconce. Any attractive 1" hardwood may be used for this project. A triangle hanger or hanger of choice is attached to the back of the project.

Drill blade entry holes, and cut the inside openings of the cross pattern. Cut the perimeter pattern line.

For perfect straight edges, the shelves can be sanded using a disc sander. Use a router to create a decorative edge on three sides of each shelf. Glue the shelves in place on the cross in the positions indicated.

Apply deep penetrating furniture wax liquid or Danish oil™ to the work pieces, following the manufacturer's directions.

Patterns

*Note: The patterns on this page have been reduced by 50%. For a full size pattern, enlarge 200%

Cross Sconce, cross.
Cut 1 from 1" material.

Cross Sconce, shelf.
Cut 2 from 1" material.

Cross Sconce, diagram for shelf positions.

5.4 Compound-Cut Candle Stand

The compound-cut method is used to make the main upright of the candle stand. Pieces of wood can be laminated to get the required thickness of 2.6" for this piece.

Apply wood glue to the connecting surfaces, join the pieces, and apply clamps.

Cut two oversized wood pieces on the scroll saw.

Fold the pattern on the center line. Cover two adjoining sides of the work piece with masking tape and apply the pattern using temporary bond spray adhesive or glue stick. Smooth down the pattern on the work piece.

Use the disc sander to sand the two ends of the work piece up to the pattern lines.

Using a large size blade, make two continuous cuts along the pattern lines on one side of the work piece. Depending on the wood you are using, progress may be slow in this thickness. Be patient and use a steady feed rate without forcing the blade. Use a vacuum nozzle to remove the wood dust from the cuts.

Replace the waste pieces and secure with clear packing tape.

Make the second set of cuts in the same manner. Remove the waste pieces of wood to reveal the stand piece.

Making the Overlays

Stack four layers of 1/8" hardwood, plywood, or MDF for the overlays. Use dark colored wood or stain the completed overlays before assembly. The straight edges of the stack can be sanded using a disc sander. Drill blade entry holes and cut the inside openings. The overlay design has some fragile fretwork cuts in parts of the pattern. Be careful not to catch and break these pieces during the cutting and sanding processes. Using small beads of wood glue, attach the overlays to the sides of the main structure.

Drill the blade entry holes of the overlay stack.

Thread the blade and make the fret cuts of the overlays.

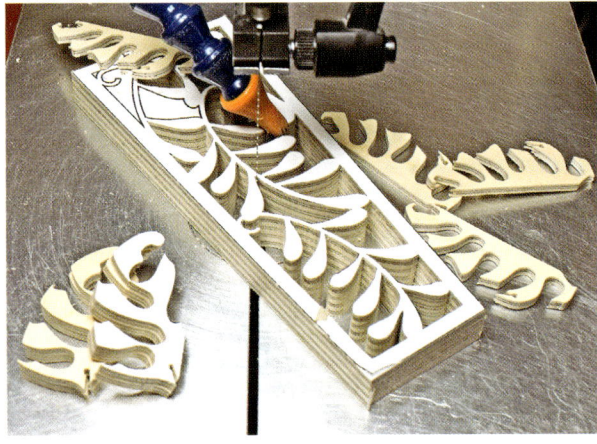

Remove the pattern and insert a scraper blade between the layers to separate the overlay pieces.

Making the Base and Top Piece

Use 1.5" hardwood for the larger base and 1" hardwood for the smaller base and the top piece. A decorative edge is applied to each of these work pieces using a router and a cove bit.

~~~~~

To finish, assemble the candle stand using wood glue. Secure the small base on top of the large base. Center the main structure onto the bases and complete the assembly with the top platform. Rubber bumpers or felt can be attached underneath the candle stand to protect the surface it will be displayed on.

Patterns

Compound-Cut Candle Stand, overlay.
Cut 4 from 1/8" material.

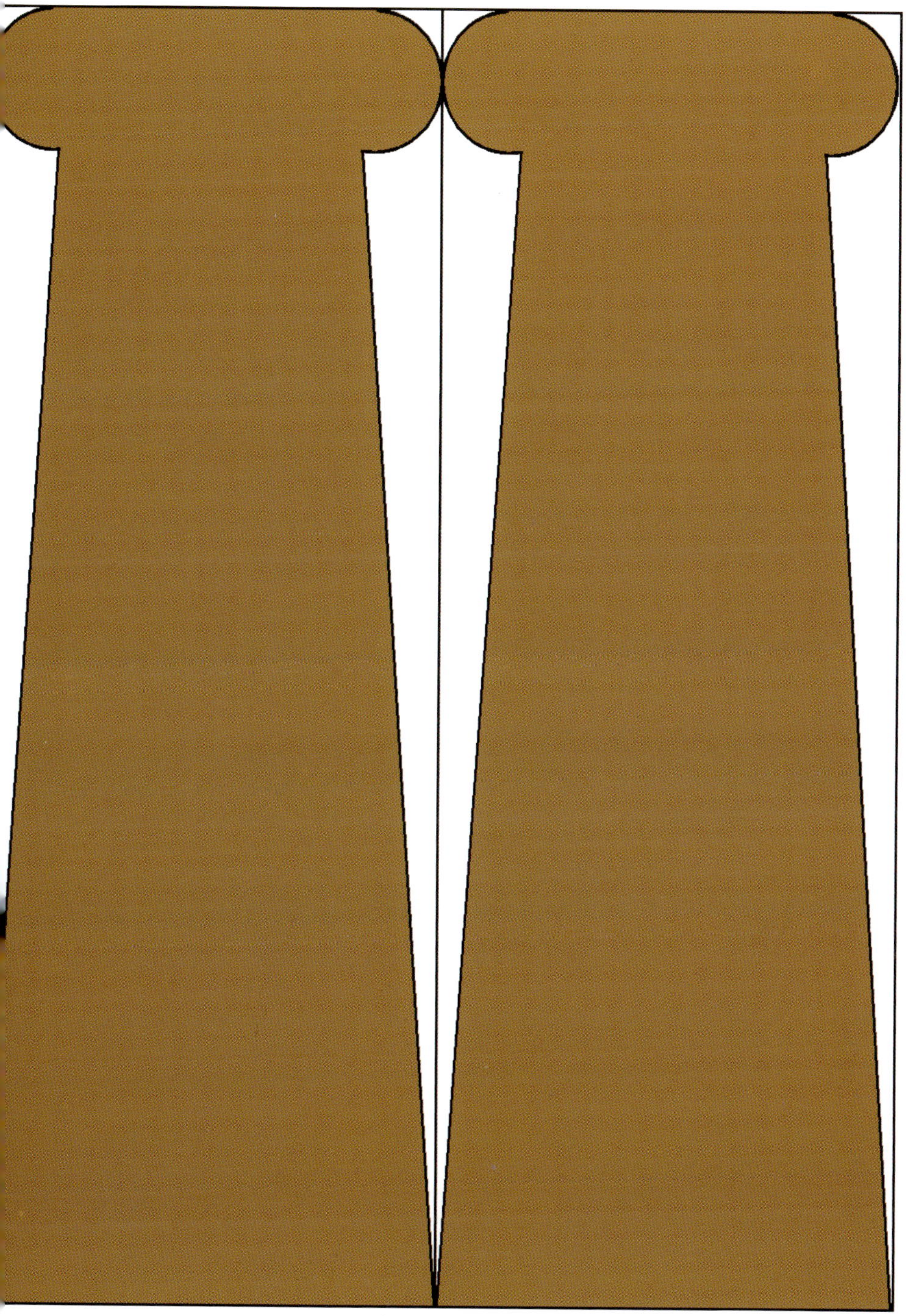

Compound-Cut Candle Stand, upright. Cut 1 from 2.6" square material.

Compound-Cut Candle Stand, large base. Cut 1 from 1.5" material.

Inner shape:
Compound-Cut Candle Stand, small base. Cut 1 from 1" material.

Compound-Cut Candle Stand, top. Cut 1 from 1" material.

5.5 Patio Candle Lamp

This attractive candle lamp is ideal for a patio table or on a low table on the deck, surrounded by foliage. A battery operated pillar candle or one of the round paper luminaries from *Chapter Two* is used inside the lamp. The project can be made from hardwood, but I chose MDF for the majority of the work pieces and used mat black spray paint to imitate the metal appearance of an outside lamp, while clear acrylic on the inside of the lamp panels suggests glass.

The material thickness required are 1/4" for the lamp panels, 1/8" for the lid inner, 1" for the base, and 1.5" for the lid. The lid handle is cut from 2" square wood and the compound cut method is used.

Join together two layers of wood for each set of panels. Sand the straight edges of all the work pieces for the project using the disc sander.

Drill blade entry holes and cut the inside openings.

Cut the slots of the lamp panels on the pattern lines and then separate the stacked layers.

Fit the panel pieces together to test the fit. The pieces should fit neatly and firmly. Widen the slot openings on the scroll saw if needed. Only cut away small amounts of wood at a time and test the fit until you are satisfied with the panel assembly. Test fit the lid inner work piece in the opening of the lamp assembly.

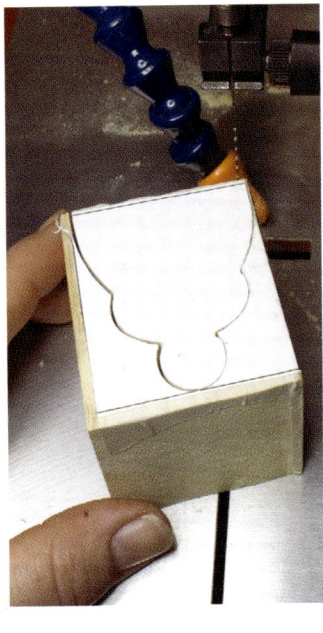 

To make the lid handle, cover two adjoining sides of the work piece with masking tape, fold the pattern on the center line, and apply the pattern using temporary bond spray adhesive or glue stick. Use the disc sander to sand the straight edge of the work piece up to the pattern line. Make a continuous cut along the pattern line on one side of the work piece. Use a vacuum nozzle to remove the wood dust from the cut.

Replace the waste piece and secure it with clear packing tape.

Make the second cut in the same manner. Remove the waste pieces of wood to reveal the lid handle.

 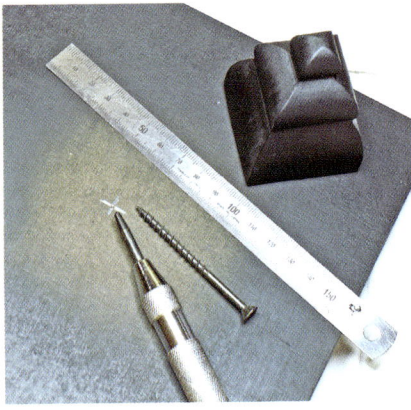 

Create a decorative edge for the lid using a router and a cove bit. The edge of the base is left plain. Apply several layers of mat black spray paint to all the work pieces. Refer to the "Basics" section of *Chapter One* for tips on successful spray painting.

The lid handle is secured to the lid by means of a 2" long wood screw that is driven all the way through the lid and into the bottom of the handle. Mark the center point on the inside of the lid using a center punch. Also mark the center of the handle.

Choose a drill bit with a diameter slightly smaller than that of the wood screw and drill a hole through the center of the lid and 1/2" into the lid handle. Use a countersink bit on the inside of the lid to prevent the head of the screw from protruding above the wood surface. Screw the handle onto the lid.

Center and glue the lid inner to the inside of the lid and apply clamps. Apply another layer of mat black spray paint to the inside surface of the lid.

Preparing the Acrylic Panels

To prepare the acrylic panels, use the pattern provided. Clear or frosted acrylic of 3/32" or 1/8" thick is required.

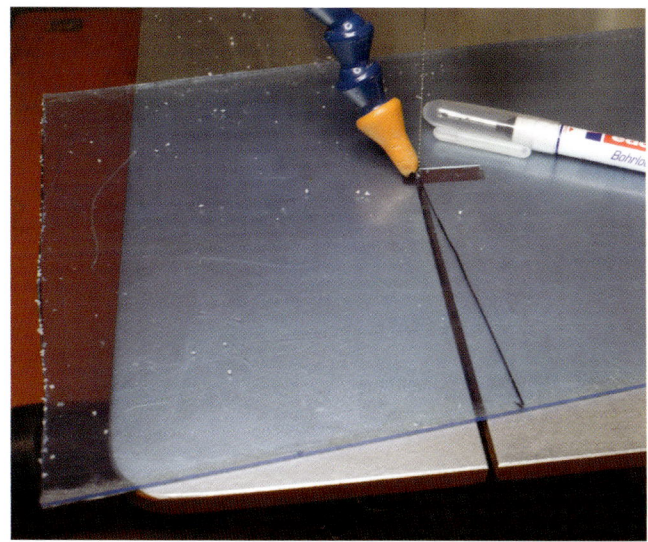

A thin-tipped permanent marker and a ruler can also be used to draw the cut lines on the protective masking film of the acrylic. Cut the pieces oversized, using a fine regular tooth blade.

Use pieces of thin double-sided tape in the corners to stack the four layers of acrylic.

Sand the stack up to the lines using the disc sander. Pry apart the layers and use fine grit sandpaper to remove any stray bits of acrylic from the sanded edges.

~~~~~~~~~

To finish, remove the protective masking film and position a piece of acrylic on the inside of each lamp panel. Apply clear silicone to secure the acrylic to the wood. Apply clamps and allow the silicone to dry, following the manufacturer's directions for the drying time required.

Reassemble the lamp panels. If the pieces do not fit firmly, use a toothpick to apply small beads of cyanoacrylate glue (CA glue or superglue™) in the slot openings and apply clamps. Use wood glue or CA glue to adhere the assembly on to the base. Place a heavy weight on top of the assembly or apply large clamps. Set the project aside for the glue to dry.

Patterns

Patio Candle Lamp, panel with top slots. Cut 2 from 1/4" material.

Patio Candle Lamp, acrylic panels. Cut 4 from 3/32" or 1/8" clear or frosted acrylic.

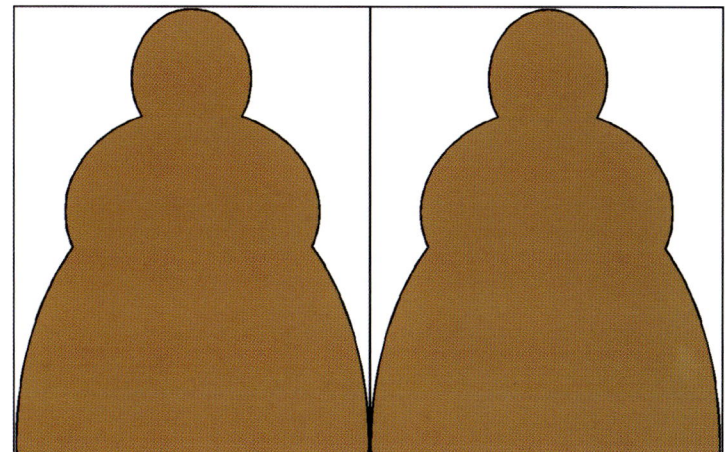

Patio Candle Lamp, lid handle. Cut 1 from 2" square material.

Patio Candle Lamp, panel with bottom slots. Cut 2 from 1/4" material.

Outer shape:
Patio Candle Lamp, lid. Cut 1 from 1.5" material.

Middle shape:
Patio Candle Lamp, base. Cut 1 from 1" material.

Inner shape:
Patio Candle Lamp, lid inner. Cut 1 from 1/8" material.

Chapter 6

Layered Projects

6.1 Layered Arch

6.2 Layered Pyramid

6.3 Layered Christmas Tree

6.4 Layered Snowman

Lighted arches, Christmas trees, and pyramids are popular during the Christmas season and are displayed on a mantle or windowsill. The double-layered projects are illuminated by a strand of fifteen or twenty Christmas lights attached to the back of the front layer. Christmas lights, also known as fairy lights or mini lights, are available as incandescent or LED options and can be electric or battery operated.

Baltic birch plywood of 1/8" or 1/4" thickness works best for these projects, but other types of plywood can also be used. The layered projects are freestanding and are designed so that the pieces fit into slotted feet. This makes it easy to take the projects apart to be stored flat when not in use. Be careful not to cut the slots in the layers and feet oversized; the fit should be firm for a sturdy project. I recommend that the slot cuts be made inside the pattern lines, and then made larger a little bit at a time until you have achieved a firm fit.

Sticky putty is handy to position the lights and wire. Hold down clips or wire saddles may be used to aid in keeping the wire in place. A hot glue gun with clear glue is used to attach the light strand and the clips behind the front layer. With the use of Christmas lights, there are some safety precautions to follow. Refer to lighting options in *Chapter 1.11* for more details.

6.1 Layered Arch

The slots of the project are designed for 1/8" wood. If you decide to use 1/4" wood for a sturdier layered arch, simply adjust the slot sizes accordingly.

Using a blade cutter and ruler, cut the pattern pieces on the dashed lines and join the pieces with clear cellotape™.

Cover the wood with a layer of masking tape. Apply the patterns to the tape using your method of choice.

If you choose to use 1/8" wood, stacking the work piece on top of a layer of scrap wood has certain advantages. It provides support for the work piece, reducing the risk of breaking fragile pieces. It also allows for more controlled cutting of thin material, making the cutting process easier. There will also be less sanding to do afterwards, as most of the burrs will be on the scrap layer at the bottom. (Attach the work piece using pieces of thin double-sided tape.)

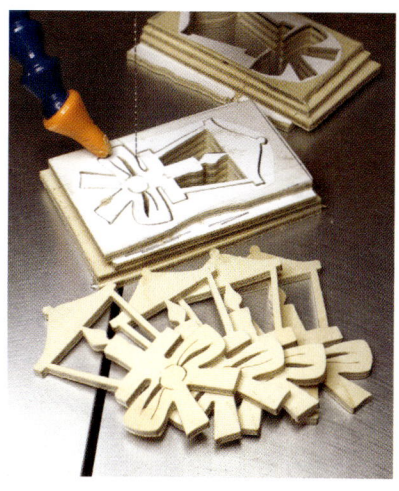

The curved arch shapes can be cut on the scroll saw or sanded up to the perimeter pattern lines using a disc sander.

To provide stability for the fragile areas while you are cutting, replace the waste cutouts in the work piece and secure them using clear tape at the top and bottom of the stack.

Stack cut the lamp overlays and the feet. First make the fret cuts of the overlays and then cut the perimeter line. If preferred, you can cut fourteen lamp overlays instead of seven and attach them to the back arch layer as well. For more tips on cutting delicate areas in a design, refer to the "Basics" section of *Chapter One*.

Use small beads of wood glue and refer to the overlay placement guide when gluing the lamp overlays on to the front layer. Apply your finish of choice to all the work pieces. I used several layers of clear spray varnish.

A strand of twenty lights is required for this project. Turn over the front arch layer and refer to the light placement guide to attach the light strand. Use sticky putty to temporarily position the lights and wire. Try to position the strand so that the wire is not visible from the front of the project. Connect the lights to the power source and make adjustments as needed. Glue down the light assembly one area at a time using a hot glue gun with clear glue. Remove the sticky putty as you progress.

Patterns

*Note: The patterns on this page have been reduced by 50%. For a full size pattern, enlarge 200%

Layered arch, back layer. Cut 1 from 1/8" material.

Layered arch, back layer. Cut 1 from 1/8" material.

Layered arch, foot.
Cut 2 from 1/8" material.

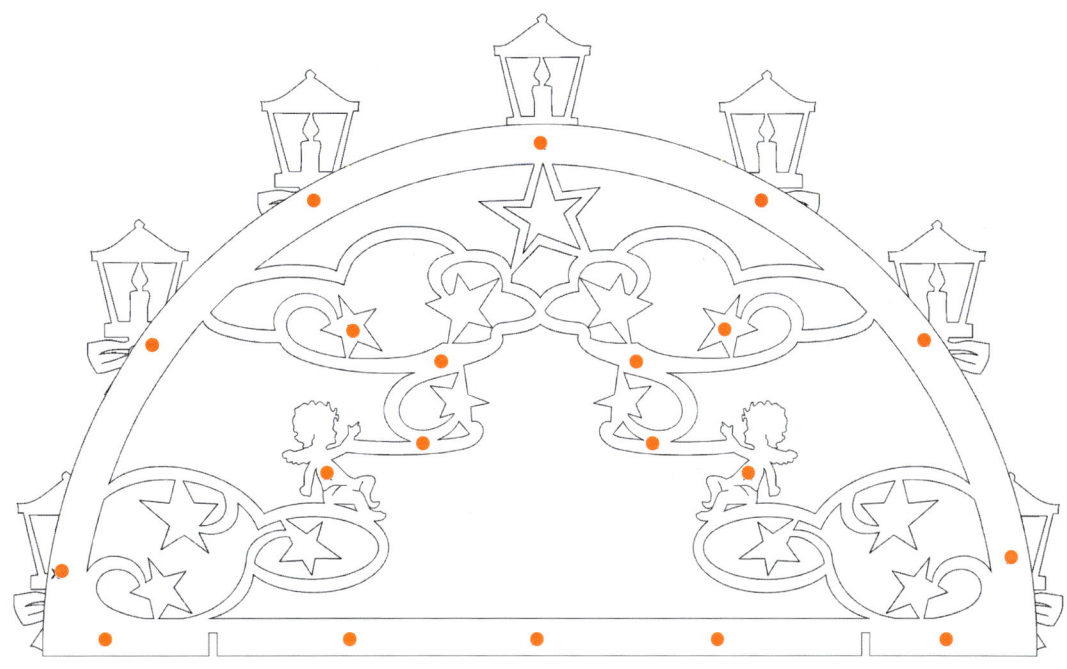

Layered arch, light placement guide

Layered arch, overlay. Cut 7 or 14 from 1/8" material.

Layered arch, overlay placement guide

6.2 Layered Pyramid

This project has two identical layers that are stack cut. Use thin strips of double-sided tape or your method of choice to join the two work pieces. Cover the surface of the top layer with masking tape and attach the pattern on top of the tape. Drill the blade entry holes. The straight edge at the bottom of the project can be sanded using a disc sander.

The design around the edge of the project is quite fragile, so take extra care not to break any pieces when separating the layers and sanding them by hand. For more information on sanding fragile pieces, refer to the "Basics" section in *Chapter One*. Finish the work pieces using your method of choice.

A strand of twenty lights is required for this project. To attach the lights to the project, refer to the light placement guide in the pattern section. Use the same procedure as described for the Layered Arch in 6.1.

First cut the inside openings of the pattern.

Cut the perimeter pattern line.

Patterns

*Note: This pattern has been reduced by 50%. For a full size pattern, enlarge 200%

Layered pyramid. Cut 2 from 1/8" material.

Layered pyramid, foot. Cut 2 from 1/8" material.

Layered pyramid, light placement guide

6.3 Layered Christmas Tree

Parts of this design are the same for the front and back layers and can be stack cut. Join the two work pieces using small pieces of thin double-sided tape. Attach the back pattern piece to the stack.

Drill the blade entry holes for the stars around the edge of the pattern, and the bells and ribbon. Make these fret cuts and cut the perimeter line of the pattern through both work piece layers. Detach the bottom work piece by carefully inserting a scraper blade between the layers and prying them apart.

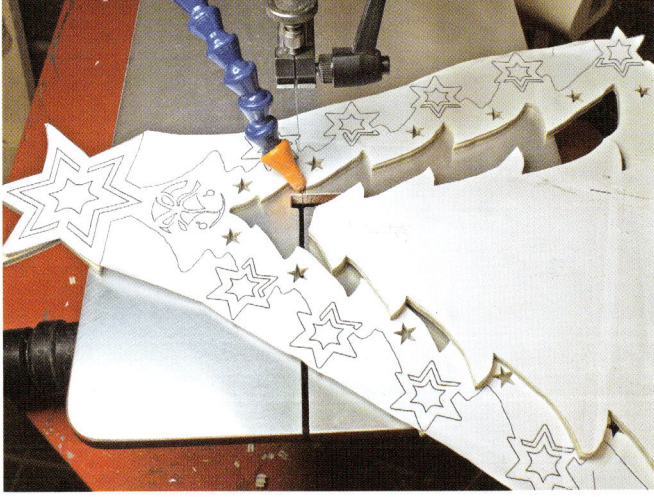

Using scissors, cut portions of the front pattern piece on the perimeter line so that the pattern can be lined up with the cut edges of the wood. Since there are no intricate inside cuts to be made for the front pattern, I simply attached the pattern to the wood with a few strips of thin double-sided tape. Drill a blade entry hole and cut the large inside opening of the front pattern. Drill the remaining blade entry holes for the back pattern and make the inside cuts.

~~~~~

To finish, a strand of twenty lights is required for this project. Attach the lights using the same procedure as described for the Layered Arch in 6.1. Refer to the light placement guide in the patterns section.

Patterns

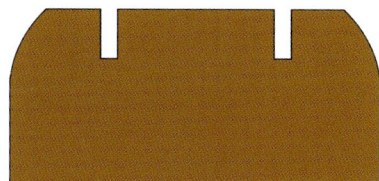

Layered Christmas tree, foot.
Cut 2 from 1/8" material.

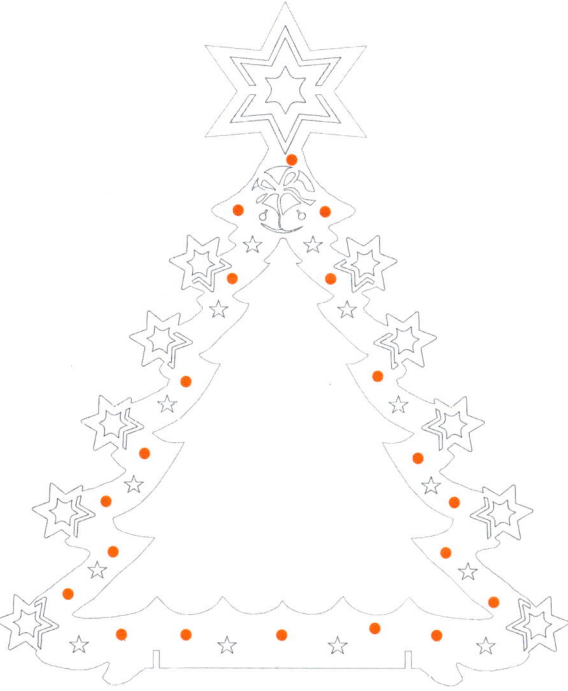

Layered Christmas tree, light placement guide.

*Note: These two patterns have been reduced by 50%. For a full size pattern, enlarge 200%

Layered Christmas tree, front layer. Cut 1 from 1/8" material.

Layered Christmas tree, back layer. Cut 1 from 1/8" material.

6.4 Layered Snowman

By omitting the Christmas lights, this project can be used as a candle stand. It may also be illuminated by arranging tea lights or votives on the base. The layered snowman requires 1/4" plywood or hardwood. Mine is made from marine plywood to which two thin layers of mat white spray paint was applied. Parts of the design are the same for the front and back layers and can be stack cut. Join the two work pieces using small pieces of thin double-sided tape. Attach the back pattern piece to the stack.

Drill the blade entry holes for all the fret openings excluding the snowman portion of the design.

Cut the inside openings and then cut the perimeter line of the pattern through both work piece layers. Separate the two layers.

Using scissors, cut portions of the front pattern piece on the perimeter line so that it can be lined up with the cut edges of the wood.

Drill the remaining blade entry holes for the back pattern and make the inside cuts.

~~~~~

To finish, cut the base. Ensure that the slots in the base are not cut oversized, as a firm fit is required for a sturdy project. A strand of fifteen or twenty lights is required for this project. To attach the lights to the project, use the same procedure as described for the Layered Arch in 6.1.

Patterns

Layered Snowman, front. Cut 1 from 1/4" material.

Layered Snowman, back. Cut 1 from 1/4" material.

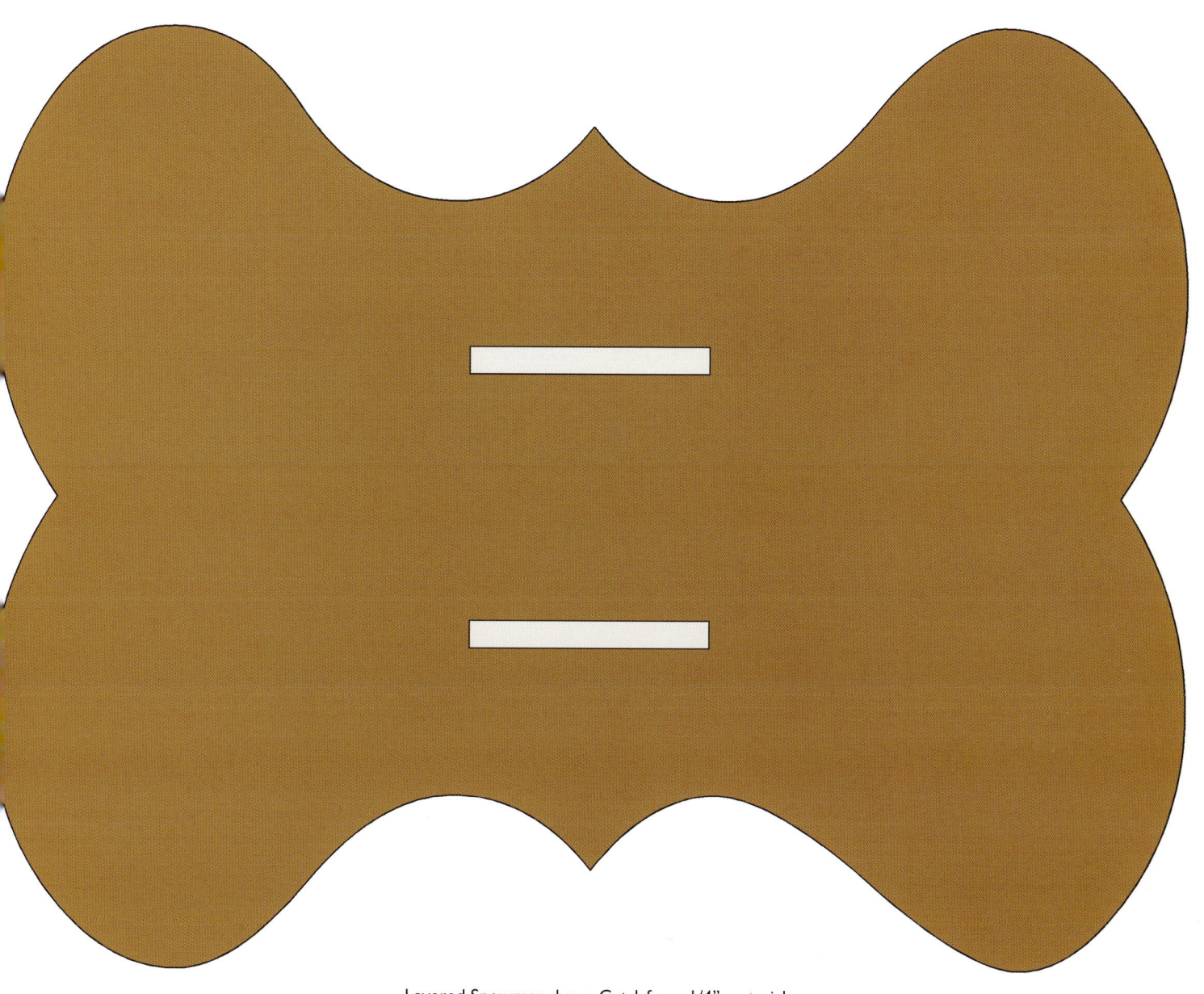

Layered Snowman, base. Cut 1 from 1/4" material.

Layered Snowman, light placement guide.

Decorative Touches

7.1 Lighted Mantle Clock

7.2 Lighted Christmas Presents

7.1 Lighted Mantle Clock

This elegant three-dimensional clock is twenty-two inches tall and consists of two box-style units with routed wood pieces as a base, divider, and top. Decorative overlays add to the attractiveness of the project.

I chose a combination of MDF and clear pine for the work pieces and applied several layers of antique ivory spray paint. For a natural look, hardwood or plywood may be used. A 3.5" clock insert is required for the project. As an alternative, clock numbers are provided in the patterns section in case you prefer to use a quarts mechanism with hands. Cut the clock numbers from 1/8" wood. A light fitting in the mid-divider illuminates the inside of the display unit. Be sure to use a low wattage miniature incandescent light bulb or a low output LED light bulb.

Using 1/4" material, construct the two box units. To make the clock box, cut the straight edges of the front, back, and side pattern pieces. For perfectly straight edges, a disc sander can be used to sand the work pieces. An opening is cut in the back piece. Use a center punch to make a mark in one corner of the inner pattern line of the back work piece.

Drill a blade entry hole on this mark using a very small diameter drill bit. I recommend a 1/32" diameter bit or smaller.

Thread a number 2/0 blade and make one continuous cut on the pattern line.

Replace the cut piece in the opening and secure with masking tape.

Use calipers to measure the back of your clock insert.

Draw the circle for the insert opening on the front work piece using a compass.

Cut the clock insert opening.

Glue up the clock box with the front and back pieces overlapping the sides.

Once the glue has dried, lightly sand the sides of the clock box and display box on the disc sander to remove any glue residue.

Making the Display Box

To make the display box, cut the straight edges of the front, back, and side pattern pieces, or sand them on the disc sander. Assemble the display box with the front and back pieces overlapping the sides. Glue up the work pieces.

~~~~~

Use 1/8" material to cut the retaining strips, top decoration overlay, and the six corner overlays, which are stack cut, and cut the top decoration from 1/4" wood.

The pieces for the top, mid-divider, and bases can be cut on the scroll saw or on a table saw. I cut theses pieces oversized and sanded the edges on the disc sander. Use 1" wood for these pieces with the exception of the larger base, where 2" wood is used. A decorative edge is created with a router and a cove bit. I left the edge of the larger base plain.

Sand all the work pieces by hand. Apply masking tape to parts of the joining surfaces of the work pieces, so that raw wood is exposed for the glue to adhere adequately when the pieces are assembled.

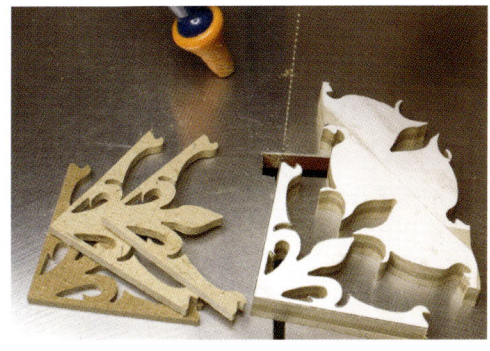

Stack cut the six corner overlays from 1/8" material.

Apply several coats of antique ivory spray paint to all the work pieces. Allow each coat to dry thoroughly before applying the next and use 500-grit sandpaper to sand the surfaces in between paint layers.

Completing the Clock Box

Cut a hole for the lamp holder in the center of the mid-divider. Adjust the circle on the pattern to match the diameter of the lamp holder you are using. Aim for a snug fit where no glue is required.

Glue the corner overlays on to the four corners of the clock box and the top corners of the display box. Glue the overlay on to the top decoration. Refer to the assembly diagram and glue up the project using wood glue.

Glue the two retaining strips for the backing in place.

Drill the holes for two turn buttons to be fitted to the top and bottom of the back piece.

Fit the turn buttons to the back piece.

Connect the electric wires to the lamp holder and insert the holder in the opening.

The mid divider with the lamp holder inserted.

Assemble the pieces one at a time and place a heavy on top of the assembly for the glue to dry.

Glue the top decoration in place.

Remove the backing from the clock box and drill a hole in one corner for the electric cord.

A back view of the completed clock box.

Fit a plug to the electric cord and insert a low wattage, miniature incandescent light bulb or a low-output LED light bulb in lamp holder.

Illuminate a special ornament in the display box.

Patterns

Mantle clock and display stand, display box front. Cut 1 from 1/4" material.

Mantle clock and display stand, display box side. Cut 2 from 1/4" material.

Mantle clock and display stand, overlay. Cut 6 from 1/8" material.

Mantle clock and display stand, clock box back. Cut 1 from 1/4" material. Use the outline to cut a solid piece of the same size and mark the center, for the clock box front

Mantle clock and display stand, clock box retaining strip. Cut 2 from 1/8" material.

Outer shape:
Mantle clock and display stand, display box back.
Cut 1 from 1/4" material.

Inner shape:
Mantle clock and display stand, clock box side.
Cut 2 from 1/4" material.

Mantle clock and display stand, top decoration. Cut 1 from 1/4" material.

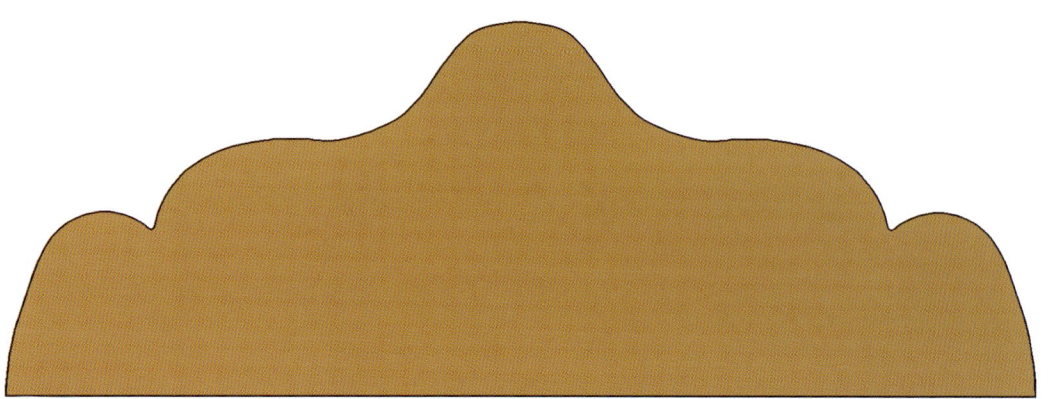

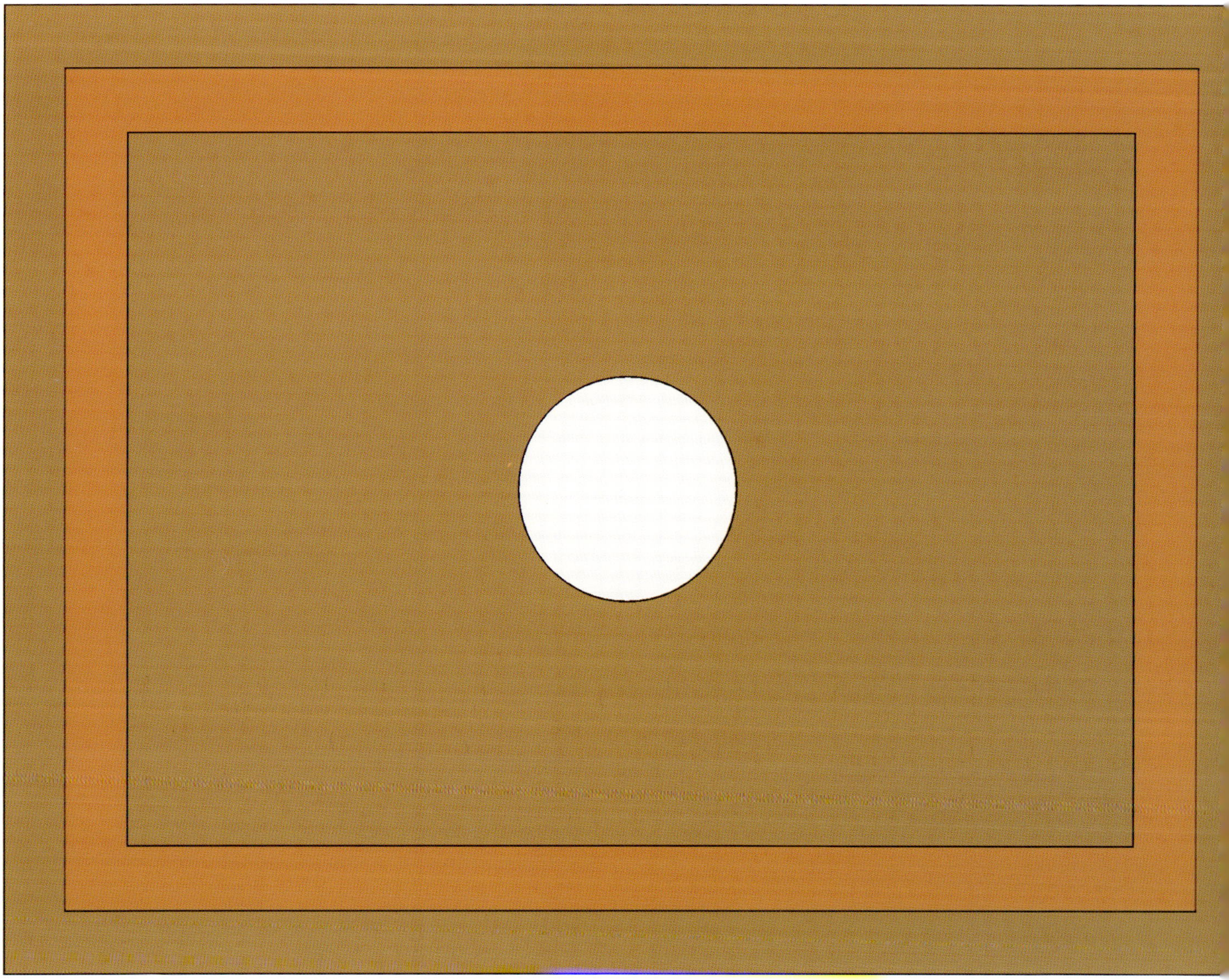

Outer shape:
Mantle clock and display stand, large base. Cut 1 from 2" material.

Middle shape:
Mantle clock and display stand, base. Cut 1 from 1" material.

Inner shape:
Mantle clock and display stand, mid divider (and top). Cut 1 from 1" material. Use the outline to cut a solid piece for the top.

Mantle clock and display stand, top decoration overlay. Cut 1 from 1/8" material.

Mantle clock and display stand, optional clock numbers. Cut from 1/8" material.

Mantle clock and display stand, assembly diagram

7.2 Lighted Christmas Presents

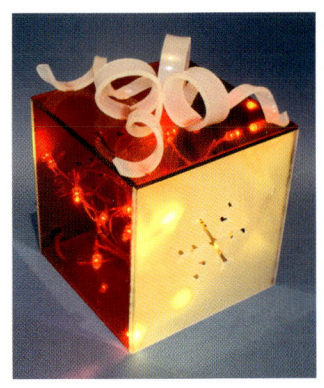

Use 1/8" acrylic to make this project. Do not remove the protective masking film until you are ready to do the assembly. If preferred, acrylic can be stacked on top of scrap plywood. It can also be sandwiched between two layers of plywood. This method reduces the problem of the plastic melting due to heat generated by the friction of the blade and the result is a clean and smooth cut surface. The boxes can be made of one color acrylic or a combination of colors. There are two designs to choose from for the front and back panels.

Special adhesives are available for bonding the acrylic work pieces. Strips of masking tape are essential to keeping the pieces in place while you line them up and to keep them in place while the adhesive dries. The drying time for different acrylic adhesives vary and can be as long as twenty four to forty eight hours. Refer to the "Basics" section in *Chapter One* for tips on drilling, cutting, and gluing acrylics.

The ribbon and bow decorations are made by heating strips of acrylic and shaping them by hand or with the aid of a broomstick or dowel. A strand of fifteen or twenty Christmas lights is placed loosely inside the completed box for a magical effect. Place the boxes around the Christmas tree or display them on a mantle or shelf.

With the use of Christmas lights there are some safety precautions to follow. Refer to lighting options in *Chapter 1.11* for more details.

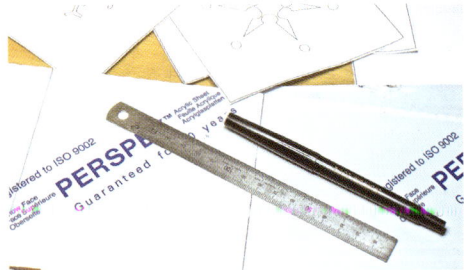

Measure the work pieces required and draw lines on the acrylic using a permanent marker.

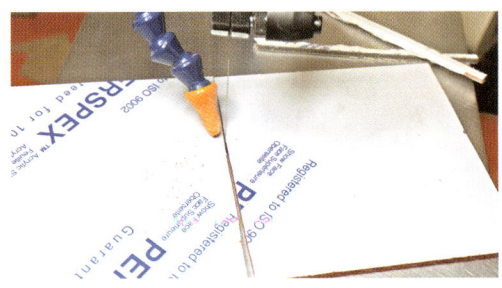

Use a fine-toothed regular blade and cut the work pieces.

Tip

IF YOU are making more than one box, add the extra pieces to the stack. If the masking film has lifted in places, it can be removed and replaced with a layer of masking tape. Use a disc sander to sand all the straight edges of the work pieces up to the pattern lines.

Stack the work pieces for the front and back pattern using strips of thin double-sided tape. Do the same for the side work pieces.

Apply the patterns on to the protective masking film of the acrylic, using glue stick or temporary bond spray adhesive.

Drill the blade entry holes for the snowflake design of the front and back pieces.

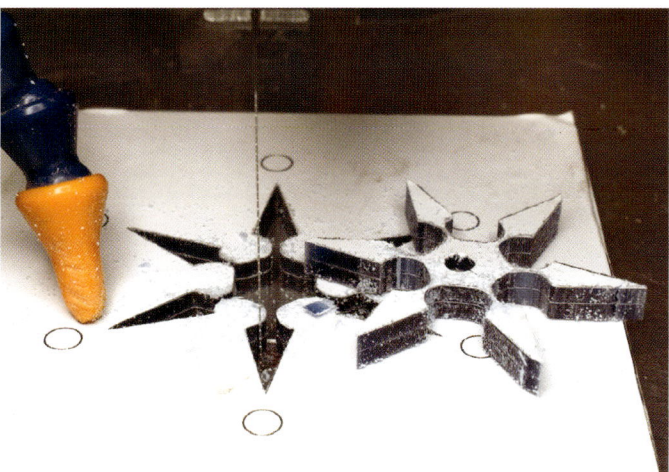

Thread a fine-toothed regular blade and cut the designs of the front and back pieces. Pry apart the layers of each stack and use fine grit sandpaper to remove any stray bits of acrylic from the sanded edges.

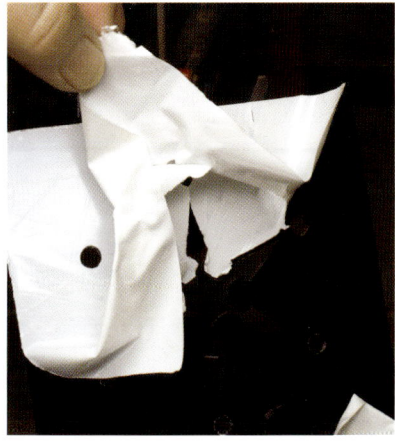

Remove the patterns and the protective masking film from the work pieces.

Needle files may be used to carefully clean out the fret cuts.

The boxes are assembled with all the work pieces joined to the outside of the base, and with the front and back pieces overlapping the sides.

Use strips of masking tape to keep the pieces in place while you line them up and to keep them in place while the adhesive dries.

Cut some thin strips of acrylic of various lengths.

Preheat an electric oven to 212 degrees Fahrenheit, or 100 degrees Celsius. Prepare a baking sheet by lining it with heavyweight cooking foil. You will also need thermal gloves or oven mittens with heavy padding for handling the warm acrylic. Place the strips of acrylic on the baking sheet and heat them in the oven for five minutes. Do not leave them unattended. The period and temperature required will vary depending on the type of acrylic used. If the acrylic does not soften, you may need to increase the heat to 266 degrees Fahrenheit, or 130 degrees Celsius. Do not increase the temperature beyond this heat setting. Test the pieces every minute or so.

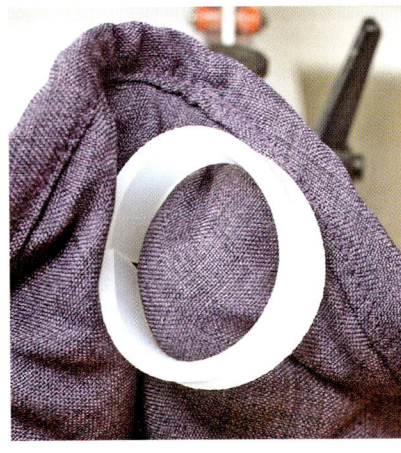

When the acrylic is pliable, remove one piece at a time and form them into round shapes while wearing the gloves or oven mittens.

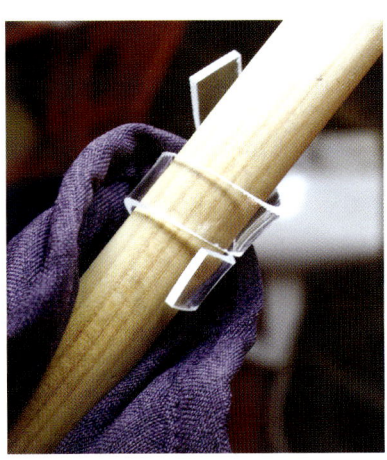

The pliable acrylic pieces can also be wrapped around a broomstick or large dowel to create round shapes and twists.

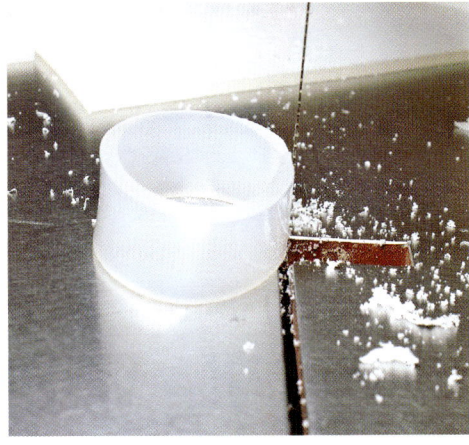

Use the scroll saw to cut a flat surface on the underside of the round shape. Position the shapes on the lid of the box and once you are satisfied with the arrangement, use small drops of the special adhesive to secure them. Place the assembly aside for the adhesive to dry.

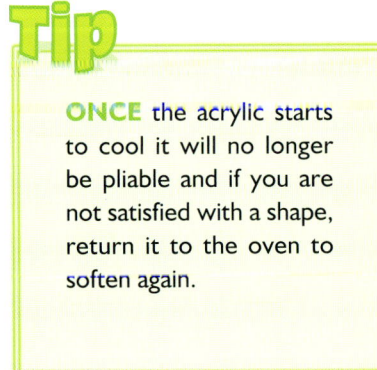

Tip

ONCE the acrylic starts to cool it will no longer be pliable and if you are not satisfied with a shape, return it to the oven to soften again.

Drill a hole in the back of the box for the light strand's power connector to fit through. Use the battery operated or LED Christmas lights so that the power connector can be fitted through a small hole in the back of the box. Place the lights loosely inside the box and thread the connector through the hole. The lights are arranged to fill the whole box and should not be compressed in the box, as this may be cause for a safety risk. Place the loose lid on the box and connect the power for an attractive display.

Patterns

Lighted Christmas Presents, front and back version 1. Cut 1 each from 1/8" material.

Outer shape:
Lighted Christmas Presents, loose lid. Cut 1 from 1/8" material.

Inner shape:
Lighted Christmas Presents, base. Cut 1 from 1/8" material.

Lighted Christmas Presents, front and back version 2. Cut 1 each from 1/8" material.

Lighted Christmas Presents, side. Cut 2 from 1/8" material.

Gallery

Tall luminary

Painted luminaries

Acrylic luminary

Fairy luminary

Painted luminaries

Assorted luminaries

Square paper luminaries

Round paper luminaries

Round paper luminaries

Assorted luminaries

Lighthouse lamp

Table lamp with overlays

Pine cones nightlight

Compound-cut candle stand

Dolphin votive stand

Fairy on moon nightlight

123

Bright sun nightlight

Cross sconce

Decorative fret nightlight

Patio candle lamp

Cherubs nightlight

Layered Arch

Layered Christmas tree

Layered Pyramid

Nativity candle stand

Lighted Mantle Clock and Display Box

Layered Snowman

Lighted Christmas presents